Commissioning Angels

Volume 1

Maximizing Our Relationship
with Heavenly Hosts

By

Dr. Ron M. Horner

Commissioning Angels
Volume 1

Maximizing Our Relationship
with Heavenly Hosts

By

Dr. Ron M. Horner

LifeSpring Publishing
PO Box 5847
Pinehurst, North Carolina 28374
RonHorner.com

Commissioning Angels: Volume 1

Maximizing the Relationship with Heavenly Hosts

Copyright © 2022 Dr. Ron M. Horner

Scripture is taken from the New King James Version®. Copyright © 1982 by Thomas Nelson. Used by permission. All rights reserved. (Unless otherwise noted.)

Scripture marked (TPT) is taken from the The Passion Translation Copyright ©2017, 2018 by Passion & Fire Ministries, Inc. Used by permission. All rights reserved. ThePassionTranslation.com

Scripture marked (ARTB) is taken from the Ancient Roots Translinear Bible by Frances Werner. Copyright © 2005, 2006. 2011. Used by permission of the author.

All rights reserved. This book is protected by the copyright laws of the United States of America. This book may not be copied or reprinted for commercial gain or profit. The use of short quotations or occasional page copying for personal, or group study is permitted and encouraged. Permission will be granted upon request.

Any trademarks mentioned or used are the property of their respective owners.

Requests for bulk sales discounts, editorial permissions, or other information should be addressed to:

LifeSpring Publishing
PO Box 5847
Pinehurst, NC 28374 USA

Additional copies available at www.courtsofheaven.net

ISBN 13 TP: 978-1-953684-30-1
ISBN 13 eBook: 978-1-953684-31-8

Cover Design by Darian Horner Design
(www.darianhorner.com)
Image: 123rf.com #126571252

First Edition: June 2022

10 9 8 7 6 5 4 3 2 1

Printed in the United States of America

Table of Contents

Acknowledgments i
Preface iii
Chapter 1 Commissioning Angels 1
Chapter 2 Erecting Shields and Governing Realms 15
Chapter 3 Collapsing Storms 27
Chapter 4 New Weapons 47
Chapter 5 Frequency Shields & Push Back 57
Chapter 6 Responding to Push Back 69
Chapter 7 The Intruders 75
Chapter 8 Building a Defense Against Lies 85
Chapter 9 Obtaining Clarity & Balance 107
Chapter 10 The Angel of the Broad Sword 117
Chapter 11 Angelic Engagement 123
Chapter 12 Calendar Seeds 127
Chapter 13 The Angel of Inventory 131
Chapter 14 Working with Our Assignments ... 135
Chapter 15 Using the Keys for Harvest 151
Chapter 16 The Hall of Treasures 159
Chapter 17 Commission for Ripened Harvest 183

Chapter 18 Commissioning Angels Script 187

Chapter 19 Angels of Advancement 189

Chapter 20 Conclusion 197

Appendix 201

Learning to Live Spirit First 201

Works Cited 209

Description 211

About the Author 213

Other Books by Dr. Ron M. Horner 215

Acknowledgments

Many persons and beings have been involved in receiving the revelation contained in this book. Without naming them, I simply thank them for their service.

Thanks to the awesome Courts of Heaven team who work tirelessly to see people brought to freedom through the Courts of Heaven and engagements with Heaven. Thanks also to my audience and supporters. May the blessings of Heaven overflow in your life.

Preface

One of the biggest obstacles to working with angels that I have observed over the last couple of years is unbelief that they exist. Many of us have been taught that angels are weak, dainty creatures that adorn Christmas trees or Valentine's Day cards. Angels and their work ARE NOT FAIRYTALES! They are real. They have existed long before mankind appeared on the earth. They have purpose. They have instructions to fulfill from the Father, and they are here to help us develop into a son or daughter of God.

In my book *Engaging Angels in the Realms of Heaven*, I gave many examples of various commissions for angels. I won't repeat those in this book, but I will stress the fact that we are uniquely equipped to engage with angels in this physical realm, as well as engage with them in the realms of Heaven. The various commissions will be italicized and will be scattered throughout the pages of this book. On many of them, an individual can easily adapt them to their situation and to their angels. Those that have chosen to trade with this ministry by obtaining this book, may also commission their angel(s) to work with Ezekiel, the Chief Angel over this ministry, as well as his commanders and ranks. This networking strengthens the work the angels accomplish.

For example:

I call the angels assigned to me to draw near. (Once you sense their nearness, then begin the commissioning.)

I commission you to network with Ezekiel, the Chief Angel over LifeSpring International Ministries, as well as his commanders and ranks, in Jesus' name, in time and out of time.

In the first few chapters, we will discuss various new weaponry we were made aware of and how to commission our angels to the effective use of them.

Then we go to other subject matter and teach on how to engage and work with our angels.

The Psalmist wrote about us in Psalm 8:1-9:

[1] Lord, Your name is so great and powerful! People everywhere see your splendor. Your glorious majesty streams from the heavens, filling the earth with the fame of Your name! [2] You have built a stronghold by the songs of babies. Strength rises up with the chorus of singing children. This kind of praise has the power to shut Satan's mouth. **Childlike worship will silence the madness of those who oppose You.**

³ Look at the splendor of Your skies, Your creative genius glowing in the heavens. When I gaze at Your moon and Your stars, mounted like jewels in their settings, I know You are the fascinating artist who fashioned it all! But when I look up and see such wonder and workmanship above, I have to ask You this question:

⁴ Compared to all this cosmic glory, why would You bother with puny, mortal man or be infatuated with Adam's sons?

*⁵ Yet what honor You have given to men, created only a little lower than Elohim, crowned like kings and queens with glory and magnificence. ⁶ You have **delegated to them mastery** over all you have made, making everything subservient to **their** authority, placing earth itself **under the feet** of Your image-bearers. ⁷⁻⁸ All the created order and every living thing of the earth, sky, and sea—the wildest beasts and all the sea creatures—**everything is in submission to Adam's sons.***

⁹ Lord, Your name is so great and powerful. People everywhere see Your majesty! What glory streams from the heavens, filling the earth with the fame of Your name! (TPT) (Emphasis mine)

Having had some tell me that we could not speak to our angels, when I clearly see that Mary engaged Gabriel, as did Daniel, while others in the Bible engaged with and spoke to angels, I find such arguments foolish and steeped in religion, especially in light of the current practice of talking to demons in our spiritual warfare activities.

I have had others tell me that we had to be of a certain spiritual stature to qualify for angels to speak to us. That is bunk! How theologically qualified were the shepherds when the host of angels came, or how deep spiritually was the young girl Mary when Gabriel came to visit? The fact is, Heaven can send who they want when they want to visit us, speak to us, instruct us, or anything else Heaven deems desirable. Let's remove our religious robes and step into what Heaven has for us. It is time we learned to co-labor with Heaven on a whole new level!

Now, follow me in this commission for our angels:

I call the angels assigned to me to draw near. [Wait until you sense or see their presence.]

In the name of Jesus, I commission you to aid me in the intake of revelation from this book. I commission you to aid me to water it and cultivate it, so it brings forth maximum fruit in my life, in my family, in my relationships, and in my business or ministry, and employment arena.

I commission you to keep me alert as I read.

I commission you to aid me to hear every instruction and nuance of expression of Heaven.

I release you to this work, in time and out of time, in Jesus' name.

In our engagements with Heaven, we were assisted by various angels and men and women in white. Those mentioned include:

Ezekiel, the Chief Angel over LifeSpring

Men or Women in White:

Lydia

Malcolm

Marcus

Mitchell

George

We are grateful for the wisdom and revelation they share. We are merely the recipients of it.

Chapter 1

Commissioning Angels

When engaging Heaven this day, Ezekiel appeared, but he was very quiet. He stood with his arms crossed. We noted that his demeanor was very stalwart.

He reminded us, saying, "The Lord God, He is almighty, and He is King forever. Witchcraft, occult manifestations, and cursings of those aligned with evil will not override this victorious King. He is King forever. He is a purifying King to those in His army. He is holy. Beyond all, He is righteous and true. It goes well with the sons and daughters of God when they recall the mightiness of this King, the overwhelming victory He stands in, and the greatness of His power that is ever increasing and without end. It is power—mighty power. Think of the explosiveness of our God. We must recall in Whose camp we are and Whose army we are in. We fight from certainty to certainty of His victory against evil.

"I am of a sober mind today because I know this piercing gaze of the King and of His battle plan. Above all things, He is to be praised. He is to be glorified and worshipped, for He is worthy.

"God is not going to strive with the self-centeredness of man's self-idolatry indefinitely. Self-idolatry is like death. It is like ashes. It is the absence of life. And there are those on the globe who have fallen to the severe deception that they are god, and there is no other. Yahweh will not strive with them forever."

Ezekiel continued, "I am speaking of those who make willful choices to follow after evil. I am not speaking of those who are caught in deception, for they are to be pitied. But there are those aligned with evil and who are agents of Satan. They will have their time and they will fall under the Judgment of a Holy God."

He went on to explain that the realm of the supernatural is transgressed by many. Many are working out evil plans, and the Lord laughs at these efforts to manipulate Him.

His eye is upon those who have chosen Him and who have aligned their hearts. Many forget to seek after truth. The work of entreating the population of humanity to seek after truth continues. New opportunities and new tactics for this entreaty are changing and will change for a coming time of power demonstrations of God on the earth, when His glory will arrive and be seen. Many eyes will be unveiled, and many will find, to their shock, their position in the Kingdom.

Our brothers and sisters are sometimes weak in the knowledge of their position in Christ Jesus, and they are burdened by the overwhelming release of lies, darkness, and arrows that try to pierce them. We must continue the work of awakening, for the Father does not desire any to be slain on the battlefield. He desires us to work with those He has given us to work with, so that casualties of war are minimal. I want to be clear that many in the army of the Lord, meaning the sons and daughters of God, have not an understanding of the spiritual nature of our King, and they are working from the realm of the soul to do the work of the Kingdom.

They must soon learn the engagement of spiritual things–
in the spirit realm from their spirit–
*for **this** is their weapon of war.*

There are streams of the Body of Christ that do this, but it needs to enlarge. That flow will enlarge. It is the plan of God that it will enlarge, and the work of this is in the spiritual realm.

Continue our declaration of grace, grace, grace, to this mountain, that it be moved into the sea. The sons and daughters of God **will** awake, but some still slumber. Be encouraged. Do not be discouraged, because victory is sure.

What do we have in our hand that is our weapon? It is our faith. It is our hope. It is our relationship of truth with God. It is our weakness when He is strong. It is our determination to love unconditionally those whom the Father loves. It is our willingness to see opportune moments and to stand in those opportunities with strength of character in Him, in Jesus, and Truth. These things will remain.

When we co-labor with our angels, it strengthens them. When we see their outstretched wings, it is a reminder of how mighty and capable they are on our behalf. The angelic hosts of Heaven are extremely important in this hour. We must work together. I was urged not to forget this and to share this with our audience:

The angels of God assigned to the earth have increased in number

Even angels have longed for these times. They are powerful, capable, and have abilities humans do not possess. So, put them to work. Commission them often. Supply them with weapons and believe in their strength. Know that our belief in what they do *is a form of belief* in who our Father is, in His position as Almighty God, and in the blueprint of His plans.

When we go to pray, we ought to strengthen ourselves with the ministry of angels. We can call them near to minister to us.

Many angels are assigned to the sons and daughters, but the necessary posture of prayer in these times requires the ministry of angels in spiritual realms.

While we are engaged in prayer, when we are engaged in courtroom scenarios of prayer, when we come and when we go, when we rise and when we lie down, these are the times that the angels of God draw near and are needed by the army—by the sons and daughters of God—to work out the plans for the Kingdom. Believing in their ministry is a form of receiving their ministry and co-laboring with them to gain the accomplishment of the plan of the King.

In a nutshell, the plan of the King is...

A victory over evil.

We requested to know from Ezekiel what he needed for himself, his commanders, and his ranks. Upon receiving insight into what was needed at that time, we requested these things from the Father. Then we began to commission him.[1]

I call the angels assigned to me to come near.

I commission you, Ezekiel, with your commanders and your ranks, with the continuing awakening of

---

[1] We encourage you to take the commissions in this book and personalize them to your situations.

the sons and daughters of God to the supernatural and to the dunamis *power of God.*

I commission you, your commanders, and your ranks for necessary warfare, victorious capture of the enemy, and the awakening of the saints.

I commission you to remove veils, disintegrate strongholds, trip up the enemy at every turn—at every crossroads, and prevent theft from fertile fields.

I commission you to strengthen the saints, carry revelation to their realms, penetrate with light, defeat darkness, and conquer evil for all those connected to LifeSpring—for the staff, for the advocates, for those aligned in trade with the ministry, for those aligned with the concepts and principles that are flowing through revelation from this ministry.

I am requesting that you widen portals of revelation for the same.

I commission the angels to protect us from our enemies.

I commission you to just go and flick the little demonic beings off the saints. Get them off, so that these saints are not battling the constant barrage of lies to their heart, to their mind, and to their soul.

I commission you to refresh them, release what God has for them, widen the portal of revelation around them, and increase the Glory realm of God around them. Help them to walk in victory. Help them with their faith. Help them with their hope. Help them with their joy, and help them to know their God. That is what I commission you to do, in Jesus' name.

I commission you to bring assistance to those taking their first steps, those just getting interested in the paradigm of the Courts of Heaven, and those we are assisting as a ministry.

I am requesting you to assist those who are launching with first steps and taking baby steps into seeing in the spirit, hearing the voice of God, operating with angels, and attempting to live their lives from spirit first and Heaven down, for these who are infants in it—who are new to it.

I am releasing you to assist them, bring ministry to them, provide whatever is necessary that they get started, and that they continue in their path, that they be strengthened in their resolve to operate by faith in this inheritance that they have received as sons and daughters of Yahweh.

I commission you to these things in time and out of time, in Jesus' name.

Ezekiel indicated how he loves these commissions.

After finishing the commission, we could tell that it was a joyful thing for Ezekiel. He looked happier, excited, and powered up when he was commissioned with all these things. But it was not just the commission...

There is a role that faith is playing in how that is translated to spiritual realms.

Ezekiel exuded, 'Give me more, give me more, give me more!' Like, 'Put me in, Coach, put me in!'

Ezekiel requested another commissioning, so we began.

Ezekiel, I commission you, your commanders, and ranks to push back darkness so that the excellence of the saint—in their work, in their life, in their occupation, in their trade—is seen.

I commission you to these things in time and out of time, in Jesus' name.

What the Father wants to do is see the sons operating in a stellar excellence so that even those in the world and those aligned with world systems will see the Glory of the King on those who are walking by faith in Jesus Christ. The Father wants to see their occupation, the work of their hands, the deliverance of their words, and the working out of their deeds—are noticeably effective—so they are noticeably containers of wisdom and are noticeableto the world as the way we should walk before the Creator of all. Ezekiel relished this.

Ezekiel said, "Yes, I like that word relish. I relish this commission to make the saints of God visibly different in excellence and mighty in their strength— in a position in Jesus Christ— to be seen even by the world. Now that's a commission that an angel likes."

For this to take place, the part that the saint has to play *is to act with boldness and courage.* Commission your angel for the delivery of the oil of courage and the oil of boldness.

I call the angels assigned to me to come near.

I commission you[2] to release the oil of courage and the oil of boldness. I know that my Father has these in vats in Heaven, and I ask you to go to heavenly realms and bring out the oil of courage and the oil of boldness.

I commission you to the work of causing the saints of God to be seen with excellence and the strength of our God, in Jesus' name.

I commission you to these things in time and out of time, in Jesus' name.

When we ascend and talk to angels, when we commission them and we are listening to Holy Spirit, our

---

[2] Know that you can adapt these commissions to your angel(s).

spiritual senses are at work. Our frequency—our vibration—changes. The angels brighten and shine, similar to how the face of Moses shone with the Glory of God. His face shining was an expression of how his DNA changed from being at length in spiritual realms and of course, being in the presence of Father.

We also commissioned Ezekiel regarding the book and product sales:

> *I commission you, Ezekiel, your commanders, and ranks for increased book sales.*
>
> *I also request increased CourtsNet purchases and conference and product purchases, as well as purchases of the conference tickets.*
>
> *I commission you to those who are being positioned by the Father for awakening to spiritual things, awakening to Courts of Heaven paradigms, awakening to spirit-forward living, awakening to Heaven down business and life.*
>
> *I commission you for these increases in sales, increases in customers, and to guard and protect trade routes for the ministry, in Jesus' name.*
>
> *I commission you to these things in time and out of time, in Jesus' name.*

We are Meant to Work with Angels

One thing that is needed for the release we are sharing is something we need to hit on and hit on again. We have heard it before, but we need to cover it again.

We are meant to work with angels.
We are meant to have relationship
with some angels.

We are not meant to do this alone, and our audience needs to hear another encouragement. They need more understanding. They need encouragement to begin, expectation, and challenge to their faith that they begin commissioning angels while operating from spiritual senses, with verbally releasing and requesting angels to do things.

The sons and daughters of God
must grow up in this.

The only way to grow is *to practice*. The only way to grow is *to believe*. The only way to grow is *to have faith* and *stretch our faith muscle* regarding interaction with the angels of God. There is so much more here for the sons and daughters of God to engage in with the angels assigned to them. Far more angelic activity in the unseen Heavens than has been seen or ever known is happening right now.

We may be one ministry among many with this message, but it is a key message for this hour. Keep pressing through. Keep announcing the Heavens are open for the sons and daughters of God to operate from. Step in to engage with, grow in understanding of, and experiences with Heaven.

Commissioning In Time and Out of Time[3]

There is another thing that should be talked about when we are commissioning our angels, which is, that commissioning should include the use of a phrase that is somewhat hard to understand, but as we practice this, we will gain knowledge of how it works. The phrase is *'in time and out of time.'* Commission angels to operate 'in time and out of time' on our behalf. (All the angels will understand this—not just ranking angels.) Maps, keys, and the phrasing and the language of commissioning angels to work in time and out of time, are all important as these days progress.

Spiritual thinking is required from the spirit man, as well as rest for the soul. We can sharpen our discernment in the spirit by practice and use. Pause to see, hear, listen, and know. Receive unction and counsel. Believe in unseen things and the protection of these unseen things that angels see on our behalf.

---

[3] You may have noticed the use of the phrase "I commission you to these things in time and out of time, in Jesus' name," already in the commissionings so far. It is in response the instructions Lydia gave us for this section.

Summary

- We fight from certainty to certainty of His victory against evil.
- God is not going to strive with the self-centeredness of man's self-idolatry indefinitely.
- Self-idolatry is like death.
- Many in the army of the Lord, meaning the sons and daughters of God, do not have an understanding of the spiritual nature of the King.
- They are working from the realm of the soul to do the work of the Kingdom.
- They must soon learn the engagement of spiritual things in the spirit realm, from their spirit, for this is their weapon of war.
- Put angels to work.
- Commission them often.
- Supply them with weapons.
- Believe in their strength.
- Our belief in what they do is a form of belief in who our Father is, in His position as Almighty God, and in the blueprint of His plans.
- The necessary posture of prayer in these times requires the ministry of angels in spiritual realms.
- There is a role that faith is playing in how the commissions are translated to spiritual realms.
- We are meant to work with angels.
- We are meant to have relationship with *some* angels.
- The only way to grow is to practice.

- Commissioning angels to work in time and out of time is important as these days progress.
- Spiritual thinking is required from the spirit man.
- Rest for the soul is also required.
- We should sharpen our discernment in the spirit by practice and use.
- Pause to see, hear, listen, and know.
- Receive unction and counsel.
- Believe in unseen things and the protection of these unseen things that angels see on our behalf.

Chapter 2
Erecting Shields and Governing Realms

This engagement began with Ezekiel, the ministry angel. We asked Ezekiel what he was doing and discovered he was busy working on the shields which were up.

We can commission our angels to engage the shields that the angels are erecting. We can co-labor with the angels to both engage *this ministry's shields* and engage *our personal shields*. Angels are building shields around the ministry, and we would benefit from commissioning our personal angels to work with Ezekiel, his commanders, and ranks to engage the shields. His ranks *are* the shields—they *form* the shields.

Shields let in things that we want in. They let in the things of God, and they keep out the things of the enemy.

Sometimes we feel bombarded, but there is nothing going on in the physical realm. This is what it may feel like to us when the shields that angels are forming are being set up, when they are acting on our behalf, when they need other angelic backup, and when other angels need their backup. Angels need to work together with other angels and with us, so, we commission our angels to work with the shields—the shield function of the ministry.

Governing Our Realm

Many humans have not understood their realms, and therefore they have not understood that they have the right to govern their realm. Part of the governing of one's realm is to establish shields of protection. This is the work of angels. Many have seen the need for protection, but few have understood that the shields also work to allow in the blessings of God, allow in the harmony of Heaven, the love of God, the associations He wants for us, the handshakes, and the agreements of people that the Father wants us to have so we all can agree.

We have realms, and we are called to govern our realm. All three realms[4] that are in a person's being are to be governed. There are other realms in our realm that intersect. For instance, we intersect the LifeSpring realm. So, our realm is working with that realm. We are helping to govern that realm. We can flow to any of those realms. We want to govern them with the help of angels. We govern them by the use of agreement with God,

---

[4] Spirit realm, soul realm, and body realm.

agreement with what He is doing, agreement with His timeline, and agreement with His blessing.

> *We can commission our angels to make trades out of our realms, to allow in what the Father is speaking about us, and to keep out what He is not speaking about.*

We can ask our angels to see to the shields regarding these things.

Here is what strengthens a shield:

- Worship of God
- Intentional alignment with His Word, spoken and verbalized
- The releasing of angels
- The request to the Father for angels
- The request of things for angels (like elixir and weaponry)
- Belief in the angels
- Belief that the Father has given them to and for us
- Belief that He has made them for co-laboring
- Belief that He has given them to us for our good
- Faith as we work with them, and that we can work with them well
- Faith that they do their job.

Vocalizing all of this is helpful to these angels who work to keep shields in place.

> *By vocalizing these things aloud,*
> *we help establish them in*
> *the atmosphere about us.*

When we talk about a person, a three-part person—they are spirit, soul, and body. If we are talking about the spirit of that person, that spirit has a realm. That person's spirit must govern their realm. They govern their realm with:

- Spiritual truth
- Spiritual belief
- Spiritual faith
- Spiritual sight
- Spiritual activity

Remember that these realms intersect and overlap. They both intersect from the innermost part (our spirit) to our soul and to our body realm (the container for the spirit and soul).

Our overall[5] realm trades with other realms. The intent of our overall realm is to trade with other realms who have righteous trades to trade with us so we can trade with them.

Ezekiel reminded us of a recent experience with one of our team members.

---

[5] Our overall realm is comprised of our spirit realm, soul realm, and our body realm.

Take for example, Tom. Tom had a trade with one of us that we were aware of. He was trying to expand the trade and we were not in agreement with the trade that he was wanting to expand. We had a problem with it. So, what was happening was his trading with us had been misaligned. He had a previous trade with us, but when he made this new trade, it was outside of the previous trade he had made. We were not willing to make the new trade, and because we were not willing to make that trade, the intersection of the realms could not happen.

What was happening was we were putting up or enforcing our shield against the trade. The transaction cannot have a resolution until we have heard back from his sphere in his realm. We believed that it was an unrighteous trade that he was trying to make—not because it was bad, but because it was outside of the boundaries of the original trade. Therefore, we were not receiving the new trade into our realm. The agreement *did not feel balanced to us.* We were being asked to give more than we were willing to give. That is a definition of being stolen from.

The frustration of an imbalanced trade created a dissonance between the realms. What exacerbated this dissonance was the lack of communication about what was willing to be traded and not willing to be traded. When we communicated to him where we stood—what we were not willing to trade, then his realm could either align or retreat. If the choice was retreat, that's not negative. We ought not put that in a good or bad category. It's a neutral category. Retreat means he was gone—he was retreating to think about it. He will either agree, or he will retreat. If he retreats, he may come back with another thing, or he may just take time to agree.

Remember the verse in Amos 3:3, "How shall two walk together, lest they agree."

The Shields

Ezekiel returned to the discussion on shields saying that we will want to commission our angels to work with *what is meant to come through* because some things are meant to come through our shield.

How will we know what is meant to come through our shield?

They will have been written into books of Heaven about us.

We commission our angels to allow into our realm the things that are written in Heaven about us:

- The words of the Father
- The books written about us in Heaven
- The maps about us in Heaven
- The potentials about us in Heaven.

We want these things in *the measured flow* of Heaven to our realms. We have a role in this to work with the angels to accommodate the trades—even with Heaven, with people, structures, etc.

Declaration & Commission for Erecting Shields & Governing Realms

I call the angels assigned to me to come near. [Await the sense of their arrival. Once we sense their arrival, verbally say:]

I am a realm. I choose to govern my spirit realm in the name of Jesus through the love of God for me through my salvation—through my redemption in Christ Jesus.

I commission my angels to make trades out of my realms to allow in what the Father is speaking about me, and to keep out what He is not speaking about me. I commission my personal angels to erect my personal shields.

I commission angels to establish shields around me, around my family, my co-workers, and those I am in close relationship with.

I ask for these shields to be erected so that evil sound does not penetrate the realms of God's people aligned with me due to the enemy's actions.

I commission angel to the use of the shields on behalf of the people of I am in close relationship with for their protection against the bombardment of evil plots and schemes so the lies of the enemy fall to the ground.

I commission my angels to engage the shields that are being erected by Heaven for my life and to see to the shields regarding these things.

I choose to govern my realms with the help of angels, by agreement with God: agreement with what He is doing, agreement with His timeline, and agreement with His blessing.

I also choose to govern my soul realm, that it may grow and learn via my spirit the things of Heaven, so that my mind is renewed in the ways of the Kingdom of God.

I choose to feed my spirit only that which is beneficial.

I also choose to govern my body realm, that it be a healthy carrier of my spirit and soul realms and that I be able to glorify God in my body.

I commission my spirit to govern my realm with spiritual truth, spiritual belief, spiritual faith, spiritual sight, and with spiritual activity.

I commission my angels to allow into my realm the things that are written in Heaven about me: the words of the Father, the books written about me in Heaven, the maps about me in Heaven, the potentials about me in Heaven.

I ask for these things in the measured flow of Heaven to my realms.

I choose to work with the angels to accommodate the trades Heaven desires with Heaven, people, and structures.

I commission my personal angels to erect my personal shields.

I commission my angels to engage the shields that are to be erected by Heaven for my life.

I commission my angels to work with Ezekiel, his commanders, and ranks regarding the shields they have erected and to work with the shield function of LifeSpring International Ministries.

I commission my angels to work with what is meant to come through these shields according to my destiny scroll.

I commission my angels to make trades out of my realms to allow in what the Father is speaking about me and to keep out what He is not speaking about.

I commission my angels to see to the shields regarding these things.

I commission my angels to work with the angels assigned to LifeSpring International Ministries to develop the shield all around my spirit realm, to strengthen it, to support it, to engage it, to keep it activated, and to see to it.

I commission my angels to allow in the blessings of God, the harmony of Heaven, the love of God, the associations He wants for me, the handshakes, and the agreements of people that the Father wants for me so we can all agree with the purposes and desire of God.

I also commission my angels to help me understand where a breach has happened in a shield so that I can work together with the angels to strengthen the shield.

I choose to strengthen my shield by the worship of God, by intentional alignment with His Word spoken and verbalized, by the releasing of angels, by request of the Father for angels, by the request of things for angels (like elixir and weaponry), by my belief in them, by the belief that He has given them and made them for co-laboring, and with belief He has given them to me for my good. I choose to work with them, so they do their job.

I declare these things in the name of Jesus Christ and commission the angels assigned to these things, in time and out of time, in Jesus' name.

Summary

- Commission our angels to engage the shields that they erect.
- Co-labor with them to both engage the shields they erect and engage their personal shields.

- Shields let in things that we want in. They let in the things of God, and they keep out the things of the enemy.
- Part of the governing of one's realm is to establish shields of protection. This is the work of angels.
- Many have seen the need for protection, but few have understood that the shields also work to allow in:
    - the blessings of God,
    - the harmony of Heaven,
    - the love of God,
    - the associations He wants for us,
    - the handshakes and the agreements of people that the Father wants us to have so we all can agree.
- We want to govern the shields with the help of angels and
- Govern the shields by the use of agreement with God.
- That person's spirit must govern their realm and they govern their realm:
    - with spiritual truth,
    - with spiritual belief,
    - with spiritual faith,
    - with spiritual sight,
    - with spiritual activity.
- Our realm trades with other realms.

- The intent of our realm is to trade with other realms who have righteous trades to trade with us so we can trade with them.
- Commission our angels to allow into our realm the things that are written in Heaven about us:
    - the words of the Father,
    - the books written about us in Heaven,
    - the maps about us in Heaven,
    - the potentials about us in Heaven.

Chapter 3
Collapsing Storms

Ezekiel emerged from between two whirlwinds or dust storms (or as some call them—dust devils) during this engagement. He appeared to have them under his hands as he walked through them. As we watched and as he put his hands downward, the storms got smaller. When he raised his hands, they got larger. We were going to need greater understanding about what he was showing us.

Ezekiel began to explain that in the vision we were looking at a storm from a spiritual viewpoint. He was showing us how capable angels are at dealing with storms. He was showing this because he had been putting out or flattening a few storms. This is the work of angels. They can collapse storms but need our help and partnership.

At that point in time, we had a couple of storms on our hands—one with a student and one with a client. The enemy brings storms as a type of weapon against us in the form of a distraction. It was coming through a hardship in a person's life that the enemy was using against the work and the calling of this ministry.

> *LifeSpring International Ministries has been called to lead the body of Christ in understanding spiritual revelation.*

Angels have the capacity to collapse realms. A storm *can be* a realm and a realm is a type of entity. It has a sentience.[6] This type of entity called a storm can be loosed upon people, timelines, businesses, and ministries to bring forward movement to a halt.

Many people see the detail of the storm without recognizing what the author of the storm is saying.

> *Very few understand they can call a halt to the storm like Jesus did from the boat.[7]*

Things are stirred by enemy plans. Remember the enemy is evil, seeking to kill, destroy, or steal from a ministry or business operating in blessing and forward movement with growth. When a consistent growth pattern comes up before the enemy, it is a vile thing in his sight. Under the focus of demonic councils, he tries to

---

[6] The capacity to be aware of sensations and feelings.
[7] Mark 4:35-41

stop it and tries to bring ruination, or digression, or a halt to their blessing and their movement.

The enemy trembles when the sons of God increase.

The sons of God are now increasing, and the enemy is terrified. So, he releases a storm against these individuals or entities. The storm has what we would call an algorithm, and this gives the storm its so-called sentience. I will get to the point. **We will need to commission angelic hosts to collapse the storm.**

In the Scripture, the storm came to deviate Jesus and the disciples from the mission at hand.

That is one descriptive nuance of a storm: **its purpose is to deviate us from where we are going.** It wants to make us go around, make us slow down, or make us stop. So, if we have a storm, it has been stirred by evil thrones and evil trading routes and trade in this sort of activity.

Ezekiel showed us how to collapse a storm, by commissioning angels of the Host of Heaven. Kat Kerr uses different language. She looses the Host of Heaven to *shred* the activity of the enemy—the activity of those involved in evil trade.

How do we release the armies of Heaven?

There are different classes of the race of angels assigned to these capacities. Some are more skilled than others. They know who they are. Operating like this is new to some in the church. As sons of God who are maturing in Jesus Christ, seeking to operate from Him by the Holy Spirit, we are given access to command armies—warring angels, the host of Heaven, the armies of God.

In fact, these are based on our assignment and where we are in the season of life we are in. There are different levels of our access to different armies.

As a ministry, someone must direct the army that has been assigned to the ministry.

Angels have been doing this as we have commissioned them. Ezekiel, his commanders, and ranks form an army, but there are other armies that are not dedicated to specifically work with this ministry, though he has access to them. We have access to them, too, but we can go through Ezekiel to access them.

At this point Ezekiel suggested we trade with Mitchell, a man in white who had instructed us many times before. So, we requested that he join us, and we invited him to help us understand.

Trading with Mitchell

We learned from Mitchell that some of what he shared with us—this ability—had been reserved for these days. He wanted us to understand not all the knowledge that is being released from the Father right now has always been on the planet or has been released to men in prior times. Some has been reserved for the days in which we are living. There is more knowledge in books that have been reserved for our future generations for the days in which they will walk. But now is the time for us for this knowledge to be shared with God's children through His sons.

The storms that are stirred by demonic powers, thrones, powers, principalities, and dominions are set against the people of God and as Ezekiel had shared, especially set against the expansion of the Kingdom.

The storm seeks to remove the ease with which we are completing a mission and an assignment.

Know that some of the things we call storms are not storms.

Some of the things we call storms are simply the uphill climb to live among the world—those blinded by the tree of the knowledge of good and evil, those not eating of the right fruit, those seeking after other gods, even self-idolatry. In their deception, they build idols to themselves. Some of these idols they built as idols of themself because they idolize themselves.

Nevertheless, Satanic activity comes against those who are breaking through to new levels of knowledge, power, and understanding. This activity comes against those also who are taking possession of released seed, harvested seed, and who are learning to build in the spirit realm as we are growing in relationship with the Father, and the Son, and the Holy Spirit.

---

*A storm sent against us
can primarily be discovered
because it is very distracting.*

---

*Our ability to collapse a storm
comes at the hands of angels.*

If we have relationships with angels, we can see how helpful this is. If we have no relationship with angels or have never used them, we can see how it is needful to begin relationship with the angels of God so that the partnership of children of men will grow into deeper understandings of one another.

This is how we feel about Ezekiel, who will know all the details of what we are doing. Even though we are not aware of him on a day-to-day basis, he is aware of us. How has this happened? It has happened over time. This is how relationships grow, even relationships with angels.

So, for a storm to collapse, we need to know that a storm is built on frequency.

---
*The opposite frequency
must be spoken to the storm.*

---
*Jesus spoke peace to the storm,
but He also commanded it to
cease and desist.*

---
*A son of God's authority
plays into this.*

Our *confident authority in who we are* to speak to the storm is one thing. Our confident ability to speak to angels **to help us settle the storm** is another thing.

There are different levels of understanding of our own confidence in who we are called to be in the spirit. As we are operating spirit forward—spirit first—and our spirit becomes aware of a storm, *we can simply release angels to this activity.*

Here is how we do it: *always in the authority of the highest name in Heaven,* do we release and commission the angels of God to bring to nothing—to bring down out of second Heaven atmospheres—all demonically run and instigated storms set against our path.

Evil storms are made of frequencies of darkness.

Therefore, we release the angelic armies—the release of heavenly light. We can release the lightning of God. We can release the light of God.

Notice what we are doing. This has nothing to do with other human beings. This has *everything* to do with demons and those working in league with demons, especially those working in evil trade routes.

We can commission angels to bring the frequency of this storm to zero— to flatten it, to collapse it.

We can even use the word collapse—to collapse its timeline in the name of Jesus. We use the name of Jesus because *it is the authority of the highest name.* Angels hearken to this. We can ask input from Holy Spirit, and we can also ask our angel, "Am I involved in a storm?"

If a storm has touched our sphere or our realm, we can commission angels to collapse the storm.

How to Know When a Storm is Collapsed

In the earth realm we will see a storm is collapsed when:

- the clouds fall apart,
- the wind stops the movement, (especially when)
- the enlargement of the impending threat is dissolved
- dissipates
- comes to nothing.

Do we see all this language that can be used in our commissioning of the angels to collapse storms? Oh, how the enemy does not want the sons of God to understand this tactic of his.

Now, just like everything taught, some will run the gamut of using this technique too often and wear out their angels. They will wear out angel armies assigned to them. Some will hear of it and never use it, while angel armies long to perform the action for which they were created. But without partnership from earth realm, they will be limited.

As always, there is a walk of relationship with God in this.

What Infants Do

Holy Spirit, Jesus, or the Father, as well as personal angels as messengers—all of these can help us understand what we are facing. To relate to them about this storm *is the first necessary step,* but here is what infants do. *They run headlong into the storm,* shouting and commanding angel armies to stop the storm when perhaps it is not even a storm. Instead, it is a test, or it is *a momentary proof of our ability*—OUR ability. Many of these things arise out of the Father's desire to mature His sons. So, pause to find out. *Is this for our maturity, and if so, how should I engage it?* Or *is this a wicked evil set on destruction that needs to be stopped?* And...

Since I have eyes to see it,
I have authority to stop it.

What we are doing is we are moving against the energy that the storm draws from, to remove it, and to stop it in its tracks.

Because this is spiritual, we
must think in spiritual terms.

Because it is spiritual,
we release the angels into the storm
to remove its energy.

Angels are equipped to know how to do this. Even when we have a lack of understanding of how it works, they understand how it works. They understand what powers it up. They understand what levels it up. They understand the trade routes that are involved. They understand the illegal legalities that are back doors and that are wormholes and that are trades with different realms that are invoking or bringing about this storm.

Whether it is a storm because of witchcraft or a storm because of demonic counsels, our ability to collapse the storm comes with the help of angels.

Sometimes a storm is pending, or it is threatening, but it is far off waiting in the wings to see the response of humans.

Here is what ALWAYS shuts down storms: love, unity, hope, worship, rest, trust, truth, and knowledge.

When God's people act from these realms, it defeats storms before they begin.

Now, Mitchell was smiling and said, "You have got to try it out.

> *Some people do not understand that, to operate as a son or daughter of God, they must engage the spiritual realm **from** the spirit.*

"They must practice. They must be willing, even in the spirit, to learn—to let the growth curve take place. Do not be afraid to begin because we are not going to be perfect."

> *Do not be afraid to begin.*

The Father has not given us a spirit of fear. That is an apprehension that we must be perfect. There was only One who was perfect.

Let me set this straight. There was only One who was perfect. His name was Jesus Christ. He had a particular mission on earth, and He fulfilled it with excellence. He dwells by His Spirit in the spirits of those living on planet earth, but the man Jesus was the only perfect man—the only perfect human. This should free us to be able to practice in the spirit with the power given to us in His authority. If we are paying attention to the Holy Spirit and His prompts, His checks, and His guidance within us, we will not go wrong.

We may have done this before in the natural, but now we need to try it in the spirit. When we know the will of God in a matter, for instance with a tornado, we can command the storm to dissipate. And because we knew the will of God was not destruction, that built confidence in us.

A storm is NOT the will of God.

A storm comes to steal, kill, or destroy.

It comes to distract. It is costly. It comes to bring with it associated anxieties and displacements.

Commissioning Concerning the Client Storm

Holy Spirit, I ask you for assistance to commission the angel Ezekiel, his commanders, and his ranks of armies in the spirit realm.

With specificity I address the storm that is trying to erupt around our client.

I commission the angels of God, when a person is engaged with our ministry, to quench the storm, calm the humans, collapse all energy frequencies, and bring them to nothing, as well as all backup plans for subsequent storms, in the name of Jesus.

I loose the angels to their task with God's light, His lightning, and His peace.

I bless this person in the name of Jesus.

I bless them with what Ephesians 1:18 refers to as 'eyes to see.'

I bless them that the eyes of their heart might be enlightened, so that they would know the hope of His calling, and what the riches of the glory of His inheritance in the saints is, and what is the surpassing greatness of His power toward them who believe.

I commission Ezekiel and his ranks and commanders to squelch the storm around them. Every time they link with technology to LifeSpring International Ministries and all its outlets, all emails, classes, coursework, Tuesday nights Mentoring Groups, or Wednesday Platinum or Gold meetings they shall have no trouble.

I commission you to do these things in time and out of time, in Jesus' name.

We prepared to deal with the other storm.

Commissioning Concerning the Student Storm

Only one whirlwind was under Ezekiel's hand, whereas before there were two. Ezekiel confirmed what was seen, so a second commissioning was released.

I commission Ezekiel, his commanders, and ranks in the name of Jesus to squelch and remove all energy from the storm that surrounds our student. I do this based on their commitment as a student to the Facilitators Training Program, to the mentorship class on Tuesday nights, to the connection they make with us as a Platinum Member, and all other connections to LifeSpring International Ministries.

I commission the angels to remove all energy from this storm that seeks to distract both the student and LifeSpring International Ministries and all its outlets.

I commission Ezekiel to remove all backup plans of this storm.

I commission Ezekiel to use God's light, God's lightning, and the peace of God to bring this storm to nothing, in Jesus' name.

I commission you to do these things in time and out of time, in Jesus' name.

If, after releasing commissions like these we still feel like a toddler, understand that practice will help us not feel like a toddler. Discernment will help us.

Father, I ask You for discernment and ask You for opportunity to practice and Holy Spirit, I ask You to prompt me to use this at the appropriate time and make me aware when a storm appears.

Mitchell said, "Tell the people **not everything is a storm.**"

Occasionally there are storms, but not everything is a storm. It takes a great degree of discernment on behalf of the individual to pause, hear, and know what to do.

Sometimes a storm is happening because we have taken off our armor.

In that case, it is not a storm. In that case, we are being buffeted by the enemy because he can see we took off our armor, so, put that armor back on.

I commission my angels to help me be aware to keep my armor on and engaged.

I commission you to this in time and out of time, in Jesus' name.

Finally, do not be afraid of the storm!

We cannot speak to command angels to remove the energy of the storm and collapse a storm realm if we are afraid of it.

Do we see how this also works with the *amount of confidence* we have? We are not speaking from our own realm. We are not thinking and we are not speaking separated or apart from Him. We are not speaking, hoping that this works. We are speaking, KNOWING that this works. Do you see the difference level in the confidence?

> *We are speaking out of the realm of the Kingdom.*

> *We are speaking from, and in the authority of, the name of Jesus.*

> *Our faith in the knowledge of who He is levels us up in the release of the angelic.*

Our enemies are aware when we speak.

> *They are aware of the degree level of confidence in which we speak.*

> *Some of our practice is going to have to be speaking in confidence.*

Ezekiel got our attention and pointed out that we needed to deal with another storm that was creating chaos. We commissioned Ezekiel to collapse that storm in the same way as was described earlier.

Ezekiel, I commission you to halt the wind of the storm. I command it to be still. I commission you to bring it to stillness and destroy all its backup plans, in Jesus' name.

I commission you to do these things in time and out of time, in Jesus' name.

We have the authority to deal with the storms *that* **directly affect** *our realm as a ministry* but *do not necessarily have the authority to address other storms* affecting another person even though they may have had some connection to LifeSpring. This does not commission Ezekiel to bring every storm down in a persons' realm. It brings peace to *this* storm—*the ones that relate to us as a ministry.*

Apparently, he was aware of other storms related to a certain person that he knew about, but he knew his boundary and was pointing out to us the difference.

We have authority over storms affecting us and our immediate family, our business, job, or ministry, but not necessarily over the storms affecting other people, even if we have a degree of connection to them.

With this, our engagement with Mitchell and Ezekiel was ended for this time.

As we read this revelation, we should allow Holy Spirit to speak to us concerning the storms we need to deal with and follow the steps described. We will have nuances to the storms we are facing, but these examples will help us as we go forward in victorious triumph through Jesus Christ.

Commission

I call the angels assigned to me to come near. (Wait until you sense their nearness.)

In the name of Jesus, I commission you to halt the wind of the storm.

I command it to be still.

I commission you to bring it to stillness and destroy all its backup plans, in Jesus' name.

I commission you to do these things in time and out of time, in Jesus' name.

Summary

- This entity called a storm is loosed upon people, timelines, businesses, and ministries to bring forward movement to a halt,
- Its purpose is to deviate us from where we are going. It wants to make us go around, make us slow down, or make us stop,

- The storm seeks to remove the ease with which we are completing a mission and an assignment,
- A storm sent against us can primarily be discovered because it is very distracting,
- In the authority of the highest name in Heaven, we release and commission the angels of God to bring to nothing, to bring down out of second Heaven atmospheres, all demonically run and instigated storms set against our path,
- We release the angelic armies—the release of heavenly light,
- We can release the lightning of God,
- We can release the light of God,
- Because it is spiritual, we release the angels into the storm to remove its energy,
- We can commission angels to bring the frequency of this storm to zero—to flatten it, to collapse it,
- Sometimes a storm is pending, or it is threatening, but it is far off waiting in the wings to see the response of humans,
- Love, unity, hope, worship, rest, trust, truth, and knowledge always shuts down storms.

Chapter 4

New Weapons

We engaged with Ezekiel, the ministry's angel, on this occasion, and he showed how he had been roping storms. He showed a light gray object that looked like a whirlwind or tornado. He was holding a lariat and had been using that to rope the whirlwinds and collapse them. He reminded us to commission angels to collapse storms.[8]

We can and should commission our angels to collapse storms.

He implored us, "Do not forget, we can do this more. Do not forget it! Do not forget it!! Do not forget it!!!"

In response, we immediately paused and said,

---

[8] See the chapter on Collapsing Storms.

I freshly commission you, Ezekiel, to do as you have been doing to collapse storms around LifeSpring International Ministries, its staff, its clients, its equipment, those we trade with, its outlets, and its times.

I commission you to collapse all storms that have been raised up by demons or those operating with demons.

I commission you to collapse the storms, to bring them to zero, to flatten them, and to remove their frequencies. I ask you to do this in every element, spiritual dimension, and physical dimension of those associated with LifeSpring International Ministries, all people on staff, all clients, all students, all our equipment, all our possessions, all our realms, all our spiritual portals, all our sensing, all our travel, and our finances.

I commission you and ask you to collapse these storms.

Collapse the storms around our bodies and that affect the health of our bodies.

Collapse the storms, remove the frequencies, and defeat darkness.

I commission you, your commanders, and your ranks to perform these things in time and out of time, in the name of Jesus Christ.

Wearing Righteousness Like a Robe

We must remember to not disrobe from our garments of righteousness, to wear the breastplate of righteousness. We wear His garment of righteousness.

We are the righteousness of God in Christ Jesus.

Wear it. Put it on. Take it up. Do not leave it in the closet. Think from the mentality of the righteousness of God who lives in us. We are righteous.

All of Heaven sees our righteousness in Jesus.

His righteousness is worn by His sons and daughters. The family of God wearing the righteousness of God is the remnant of God, having been fully redeemed to the true knowledge of their righteousness as sons and daughters.

Remember, righteousness trumps and rules over darkness.

Righteousness emanates a stronger, fuller velocity of power than darkness. Do not be deceived. Light rules over dark. Righteousness rules over evil so, **we must wear our righteousness**. We must watch our mouth in this. We must, in this timeframe, watch our mouth. We should exceedingly guard our lips that we speak the righteousness of God into situations, into circumstances, into developments, into the crashing waves of what God is bringing. Speak, speak, speak the righteousness of God into circumstances.

Loose the word 'righteousness' into circumstances we face.

Lydia also implored us in this lesson, explaining that when we see a circumstance, we simply stand our ground, and from the spirit and from Heaven down, we speak:

I call the angels assigned to me to come near. [Await the sense of their arrival. Once we sense their arrival, verbally say:]

I release righteousness into this situation.

I release the righteousness of God into this circumstance.

I release the righteous wrath of God to this situation, and I call alongside the righteous armies of God to insert righteousness into this timeline, in time and out of time, in Jesus' name.

Lightning Bolts

When we release righteousness into a circumstance, an angel takes what looks like a piece of white lightning, and they throw the lightning bolts like a javelin. When the lightning bolt is released, it causes people to vibrate differently.

Now think of our target. As we release the righteousness of God into a circumstance that has boiled up, when released, a light power is inserted into a situation and changes the frequency that has boiled up.

We are not loosing it to *a person*. We are loosing it *to a circumstance* because the enemy is manipulating from second heaven realms a deception, a veil, or a blanket. These are ways we say an enemy plan is afoot. When the righteous release the righteousness of God into a circumstance, the spirit realm wars with spirit and with spiritual tools. The lightnings of God are a spiritual tool.

*"He fills his hands with lightning bolts
and hurls each at its target."
Job 36:32*

Do not forget, we must release with faith. We must release lightning with faith. If we are just loosing it with our language, our verbiage, *we are not engaged rightly.* We should raise our spirit higher to the third Heaven realm and release from that place.

*Release only when
our spirit is forward because
our spirit is engaged with faith.*

We have the garment of righteousness and rather than storing it in a closet, we must put it on. It simply has to be put on in the now season. We have always had the righteousness of God in Christ, but this was a new tool, a new way to wear it and utilize it.

Fog Dispeller

Further into our engagement with Ezekiel, we requested of him what he might need. He mentioned more rope, elixir, and practice targets. Ezekiel had been working with some of the ranks with practice targets. Then he showed us what looked like a tear gas cannister. We asked what it was, and he called it a "Fog Dispeller," whose purpose was to dispel fog from the enemy, who had cloaked things and made them hard to see.

Fog Dispeller helps the people of God see what the enemy does not want them to see.

Some cautions to regard, related to this weapon, are if people would arm their angels with fog dispeller, they must be prepared *not* to agree with fear *or* hatred when the fog is removed, because something will be exposed. Remember our battle is not with humanity—it is with darkness. It is with Satan's forces. We will see the exposure of something for the purpose of prayer, for the purpose of bringing it into righteousness, and for the purpose of bringing it into alignment. But fog dispeller is definitely needed by God's people because they need to see what Satan does not want them to see. We are in a season that we need things to be exposed.

> *The purpose of exposure is to bring light to something.*

We then requested the rope and elixir for Ezekiel, his commanders, and ranks, and we also requested Fog Dispeller for them, as well as practice targets.

Then we said this,

I commission you, Ezekiel, to freely use the fog dispeller that I might see what the enemy does not want us to see.

I commission you to this in time and out of time, in Jesus' name.

Ezekiel then suggested that we tell this to the Senior Advocates, that they arm the angels of his ranks with Fog Dispeller during a session if they suddenly feel like they need more sight or to see with more clarity. We recommend this for everyone else, as well.

Summary

- Do not disrobe from our garments of righteousness.
- Wear the breastplate of righteousness.
- Wear His garment of righteousness.
    - Wear it.
    - Put it on.

- Take it up.
- Do not leave it in the closet.
- Think from the mentality of the righteousness of God who lives in us.
- We are righteous.
- All of Heaven sees our righteousness in Jesus.
- His righteousness is worn by His sons and daughters.
- The family of God wearing the righteousness of God is the remnant of God, having been fully redeemed to the true knowledge of their righteousness as sons and daughters.
- Remember, righteousness trumps and rules over darkness.
- Exceedingly guard our lips that we speak the righteousness of God:
    - into situations,
    - into circumstances,
    - into developments,
    - into the crashing waves of what God is bringing.
- Speak the righteousness of God into circumstances.
- Loose the word 'righteousness' into our circumstance.
- As I release the righteousness of God into a circumstance that has boiled up it is a light power that is inserted into a situation and changes the frequency that has boiled up.
    - We are not loosing it to a person.
    - We are loosing it to a circumstance
- Do not forget, we must release with faith.

- Release only when our spirit is forward because our spirit is engaged with faith.
- Fog Dispeller's purpose is to dispel fog that the enemy has cloaked things with and made them hard to see.
    - It helps the people of God see what the enemy does not want them to see.
- We are in a season that we need things to be exposed.

Chapter 5
Frequency Shields & Push Back

As we engaged Heaven to check in with Ezekiel, he appeared in full battle armor. We noted that Ezekiel was in full battle armor with a shield in his hand. The shield was as tall as Ezekiel (which is tall) and it had a frequency membrane stretched between two parallel poles of some sort. It was square and the poles that held this membrane, which was see-through, could collapse. He could make them narrower, or he could pull it apart and pull it wider. It is usually about 18 inches wide and is known as a Shield of Frequency. It is used in battle and is handy for warfare. Ezekiel's angelic ranks are shielding the LifeSpring with Frequency Shields.

Frequency Shields are very useful for disarming the occult weapons, which are words. Some are called spells, some have called them energy, but they have a force and a focus. They are a plot and a scheme. They are ritualistically embraced. Humans engaged in these activities are part of humanity worshiping fallen gods, and they have had their conscience seared. They have given themselves over to what they have banked on as power from Satan's realm. They are the defeated foe. These humans are deceived, and in their deception, they have fully embraced evil. This level of deception they have embraced is the type where mercy has been abandoned. They have overridden themselves and have abandoned the mercy of God.

There is a lot going on in the globe, so we need to remember that a threatened kingdom is a dangerous foe. Satan feels the threat of warring angelic hosts. This is larger than our ministry, but it is tied to the expansion of Heaven's Kingdom. So, we may feel the brunt because we are expanding. I'm speaking to many of us right now when I say, *"Our refusal to stop expanding put us on the map to be hindered."* This is the way of the enemy.

Frequency Shields are necessary.

Not all the ranks are employed with Frequency Shields. We may ask that our angels receive more, but not all angelic forces use this shield. More battle-hardened angels use these frequency shields.

These shields are not what we would give our personal angel, but we would link with warring angels for the Frequency Shields.

Father, I request a contingent of warring angels to be granted to me, in Jesus' name. I also request Frequency Shields for them.

I commission the warring angels assigned to me to the full use of the Frequency Shields on my behalf and on behalf of my (or my household's) business or ministry(ies), both in time and out of time, in Jesus' name.

For example, in an atmosphere where we are deploying warring angels and ranking angels who have achieved the use of Frequency Shields, they gather around, and these shields change shape into a large diamond shape and become linked to the other diamond-shaped shields. In this way the shields become a wall of impenetrable Frequency Shields. Placement of these shields is important.

Maps and keys are important as well—keys for maps to traverse realms. Not all angels have their keys that give them access to ways to traverse the realms. We must ask for them in their behalf. Most people have forgotten about what is under the earth. That is where the need of keys is greatest—under the earth for transport under the earth. Remember, do not think 3-D, think many more dimensions and many more dimensions which do not have time. **Deploy the ranking angels for the use of Frequency Shields.**

In our situation, Ezekiel is a ranking angel as are his commanders and about a third of his ranks have achieved this status.

Some angels are trainers, and that training is important. These are the ranks that train to achieve the use of these shields.

A portion of the following segment was inserted into Chapter 1, but the entire segment follows.

Commissioning In and Out of Time

When we are commissioning our angels, we need to use the phrase *'in time and out of time.'* We ought to commission our angels to operate in time and out of time on our behalf. (All the angels will understand this, not just ranking angels.) Maps, keys, and the phrasing and the language of commissioning angels to work in time and out of time is important as these days progress.

Spiritual thinking is required from the spirit man, as well as rest for the soul is required to allow this to occur. If our soul is dominant, our spirit cannot process the information to the soul that the soul needs to cooperate with Heaven. Live spirit forward and spirit aware. We can sharpen our discernment in the spirit by practice and use.[9] Pause to see, hear, listen, and know. Receive unction and counsel. Believe in unseen things and the

---

[9] Hebrews 5:14 "...those who by reason of use have their senses exercised to discern both good and evil."

protection of these unseen things that angels see on our behalf.

Sometimes we will be prompted to ask (on behalf of our angels) for the release of Timed Devices.[10] This is important to go along with the phrase 'in time and out of time.' We have to think dimensionally in prayer. We are learning to pray multi-dimensionally. We are learning to discern multi-dimensionally. Keep going and allow the Father to show us the mightiness of His Kingdom in time and out of time.

Covert plots have crept in to put the saints back to sleep as many are awakening in their spirit.

The work of Satan is to cover his dirty tracks by plots to put the saints back to sleep. An awakened saint to who he is in his identity and birthright and the knowledge of the victorious King is extremely threatening to Satan. This is the work of witches and other workers of darkness—those sorts of groupings that are actively working to release sleep spells.

---

[10] Timed Devices is a weapon used by angels to create havoc for the enemy. See Chapter 21 "Disrupting the Disruptor" in *Engaging Heaven for Revelation – Volume 1* (LifeSpring Publishing (2020)).

Building Bulwarks

All saints are not asleep—some have broken free! Some have incredible angelic forces working on their behalf. Ezekiel knows of these. I am aware of where the saints have plundered the kingdom of darkness to the extent that they have pushed back darkness and are now doing the work of Kingdom and the King in more territories. However, these areas are needing a further expansion. Ours is a similar one to this, and the work now is to build bulwarks, which are like a dam or an earthen berm that is to be built around the edges of the establishment of the expanded boundary area.

---

*When we dig in, the enemy knows
we are not leaving too soon.*

We are *not* backing up! We have not just made a foray to expand in our area. Now, we are building on that area. And as we build on that area that we just took back from the enemy, we are signaling to our foe that we are not leaving any time soon. We are here to stay. Therefore, he brings distractions.

---

*He will either bring a distraction
or work to put us to sleep so
we do not build.*

We should examine and analyze the situation so we can find where that is or the areas where that is. The reason the enemy would put us to sleep is to get us to stop, to cause us to lay down our building tools, lay down our weapons, lay down our identity, lay down our goal for the Kingdom, lay down our advance, lay down our dreaming plans and our hopes, and give up.

What Ezekiel was explaining was not unlike when Nehemiah[11] was building the wall, where they had to operate with a tool in one hand and a sword in the other. Then, they had to work against the release of Sanballat, Tobiah, and his group. What they were having to deal with felt somewhat like what Ezekiel was dealing with.

Realizing we needed to request a few things for Ezekiel, we paused and asked for his assistance as we made our requests. When we have that sense that our angel(s) need some things, **we can pause right there**, make the request, then commission them for the use of those items. They will even help us with the commissioning if we ask them.

> *Father, we are asking for the angels assigned to LifeSpring International Ministries, the angels assigned to the staff, the angels assigned to those aligned with LifeSpring International Ministries and what they are doing as an outpost for your Kingdom to come near.*
>
> *We ask for warring angels, also.*

---

[11] Nehemiah 4

We are asking for all these angels to be armed with Frequency Shields and with Timed Devices.

We are asking this for Ezekiel, for his commanders, for the ranking angels assigned to him, and for the warring angels also assigned to us. We are asking this in Your name, Jesus.

To the angel Ezekiel, his commanders, and his ranks, and to those angels that he networks with, in the name of Jesus, I commission you to guard time dimensions of the saints, the sons and daughters of God in Jesus.

I commission you for the building up of the boundaries of the expansion, for the reinforcement of them, and for the counsel of them.

I also commission you to set traps for the enemy, to cover all with Frequency Shields, to use the maps and the keys you have been given to work through transporting dimensions in time and out of time for the expansion of the Kingdom of God on earth as it is in Heaven, for the blessing, harvest, and fruitful supply of the saints of God, the sons and daughters who are awakened in their spirit and are awakening the spirits of others for the expression of the King, as they awaken to the new release of expressions that reveal His Glory.

I also commission you, Ezekiel, your commanders, and your ranks to your duty, for the releasing of Timed Devices, in time and out of time, that destroy evil plots, bring down thick veils, and curtail witchcraft and occult rituals.

I ask the Father for reinforcements for you in these actions, in the name of Jesus.

On behalf of the sons and daughters of God, I also commission you to engage the saints with assistance so that they may release the bountiful goodness of His Kingdom, His righteousness, His Glory, and the equity of His love to those whom the King is awakening.

I commission you Ezekiel, your commanders, and your ranks to this work in time and out of time, in Jesus' name.

Personal Commission

I call the angels assigned to me to come near. (Wait until you sense their nearness.)

In the name of Jesus, I commission you to guard time dimensions of my life.

Father, I ask for keys to the map room in behalf of my angels whom I commission to reset traps for the enemy, to cover me with Frequency Shields, to use the maps and the keys you have been given to work through the transport through dimensions in time and out of time for the expansion of the Kingdom of God on earth as it is in Heaven, for the blessing, harvest, and fruitful supply of the saints of God, those sons and daughters who are awakened in their spirit and are awakening the spirits of others for the expression of the King; as they awaken to new releases of expressions that reveal His Glory.

I also commission you for the releasing of Timed Devices in time and out of time that destroy evil plots, bring down thick veils, and curtail witchcraft and occult rituals.

I ask the Father for reinforcements for you in these actions, in the name of Jesus.

On behalf of myself as a son of God, I also commission you to engage the saints with assistance so that they may release the bountiful goodness of His Kingdom, His righteousness, His Glory, and the equity of His love to those whom the King is awakening.

I commission you to this work in time and out of time, in Jesus' name.

Summary

- Frequency Shields are useful for disarming the occult.
  - Occult weapons are words called spells, or energy, but they have a force and a focus and are a plot and a scheme.
- Satan feels the threat of warring angelic hosts.
- Our refusal to stop expanding put us on the map to be hindered.
- Frequency Shields are necessary.
- Maps and keys are important.
  - Not all angels have keys that give them access to ways to traverse the realms.
  - We must ask for them in their behalf.
- Most people have forgotten about what is under the earth.
- That is where the need of keys is greatest—under the earth for transport under the earth.
- Do not think 3-D, think many more dimensions, some of which do not have time.
- Deploy the ranking angels for the use of Frequency Shields.
- Request the release of Timed Devices.
- Use the phrase 'in time and out of time.'
- We have to think dimensionally in prayer.
- Learn to pray multi-dimensionally.
- Learn to discern multi-dimensionally.
- Allow the Father to show us the mightiness of His Kingdom in time and out of time.

- The work of Satan is to cover his dirty tracks by plots to put the saints back to sleep.
- An awakened saint to who he is in his identity and birthright and the knowledge of the victorious King is extremely threatening to Satan.
- A bulwark is like a dam or an earthen berm that is to be built around the edges of the establishment of the expanded boundary area.
- As we build on an area that we just took back from the enemy; we are signaling to our foe that we are not leaving any time soon. We are here to stay.
- Satan brings distractions.
- Satan works to put us to sleep so we do not build.

Chapter 6

Responding to Push Back

Ezekiel began to speak to us regarding similarities between the race of angels and the race of humans. Where humans believe in the victorious camp and by our word and deed, we commit to follow the way of the Lord, the following things happen:

- Angels are strengthened,
- Portals are opened, and these things come through:
  - The Mysteries of God
  - The Substance of His Kingdom
  - The Riches of His Abundance

Here is where the angels and humans are similar: Angels feel the push back of the devil.

Humans feel the push back of the devil, but this does not mean that we are defeated. *It means that we have an enemy.* I want to remind everyone, just because we feel pushed back by the enemy, this does not mean we failed. It means we have discerned a push back. So, **push back!**

*When we discern a pushback—
push back!*

We serve the greater God! Push back! And do not fall asleep! There is something about our willingness to stand and keep standing—that is *the thing that we must do.* Just because we are feeling all this push back does not mean that we sit down, **it means that we stand and we say, "I am not budging! I am standing!"** *and* **"I am standing because I know who stands with me and who I stand for!"**

Angels are similar to this. They feel the resistance, too. Do not think that they do not feel how we feel in that. They feel it, too. They sense it.

Just because we are feeling it, *does not mean we hang our head low* because we feel the push back or the resistance, or the narrowness of darkness. **We should lift up our head! We should stand on our feet!**

*Present a sturdiness in the spirit
that we are not budging,
because we know who we
are and who He is.*

*This is required.
Even if we are not advancing,
but **especially** when we are.*

There are some saints who feel the first push back of the demonic, and they flee. They run away from the battle because they felt the push back. That is somewhat silly, being that we serve a victorious King.

We cannot be afraid of push back.

We have to stand and face it. Angels know this, too. And *they stand with us* in this.

This is where the enemy gets us—
when we did not expect
the push back.

And if we would do more of expecting that the enemy is going to feel threatened by us and we can expect some push back, we will be better equipped to keep standing.

Learn to expect some push back.
Learn to expect some resistance.
But learn to overcome!
Rise up over and hold up our head
because we will be victorious!

Summary

- When we commit to follow the way of the Lord, the following things happen:
- Angels are strengthened,
- Portals are opened,

- Even angels feel the push back of the devil
- Just because we feel being pushed back by the enemy, this does not mean we failed.
- It means we have discerned a push back.
- So, push back!
- Just because we are feeling all this push back does not mean that we sit down,
- Stand and say, "I am not budging! I am standing!"
- Don't hang our head low because we feel the push back or the resistance, or the narrowness of darkness,
- Lift up our head!
- Stand on our feet!
- Present a sturdiness in the spirit that we are not budging because we know who we are and who our Father is.
- This is required even if we are not advancing, but especially when we are.
- Don't run from the battle because we feel push back.
- We cannot be afraid of push back.
- The enemy gets us when we do not expect push back.
- Learn to expect some push back.
- Learn to expect some resistance.
- If we would do more of expecting that the enemy is going to feel threatened by us and we can expect some push back, we will be better equipped to keep standing.

- But learn to overcome!
- Rise up over and hold up our head because we will be victorious!

Chapter 7

The Intruders

On occasion we may find ourselves dealing with entities that do not seek our good. These may be demons, imps, evil spirits,[12] foul birds,[13] scorpions, serpents, adders, asps, astral projected souls, principalities, and more. We have no need to fear whatever or whomever they are. They *are* defeated foes and victory over them was assured as a result of the resurrection of Jesus Christ.

However, we will face times when they seek to intrude on our space—our realms. Do not fall for the thought that if they are present, they must always have a reason. In some cases, they do, but often they are simply trespassing. They are like the dog that continually steps

---

[12] Evil spirits are lingering human spirits with an assignment against humanity. They have a demonic guard that has a principality for a boss typically. To learn more about lingering human spirits, read my book *Lingering Human Spirits*, LifeSpring Publishing (2020).

[13] Learn about foul birds in my book, *Engaging Heaven for Revelation – Volume 1*, LifeSpring Publishing (2020).

into our yard when we have made it clear to the dog and the dogs' owner that the dog is not welcome in our yard. Some simply are too dumb or lazy to read the memo: They are not wanted here!

Here is how I typically deal with demons, imps, foul birds, scorpions, serpents, adders, asps, and principalities—I don't deal with them! Not directly. I commission my angels to take care of them. They are better equipped than I am to deal with them, and they are quite capable of doing so. Do I have authority over them as a believer? Of course! But I understand that I have the authority, the angels have the might. I let them do what they are best equipped to do. I direct the traffic. A principle of leadership is to never do for ourself what another can do for us. It is the same here.

> *I call the angels assigned to me to draw near. (Wait until you sense their nearness.)*
>
> *I commission you in the name of Jesus to patrol my realms, bridges, and gates and evict any intruders you find.*
>
> *I will request for you from the Court of Angels backup if you need it to successfully evict these intruders.*
>
> *I ask you to complete these tasks in time and out of time, in the name of Jesus.*

In dealing with evil spirits or foul birds, these topics are discussed in the books identified in the footnotes. It is too extensive to deal with here.

Astral Projection

Concerning astral projected souls, I don't tolerate them either. Astral projection occurs when someone sends their soul to spy out, harass, or frighten us. We may sense an intrusion into our realms. We often will have a sense of being spied upon. The soul of the person is connected via a silver cord. We can request our angels sever the silver cord. Once the cord is cut the person performing the astral projection will die. They know that but do not expect that we know that. I may give the astral projected soul to the count of 3, to leave but in this commission, we will see that I have absolutely no tolerance for it and will deal harshly with the matter.

> Commission our angels
> to deal with astral projection.

The following commission will help us understand the process.

Ezekiel's Commission

Ezekiel, I call you near and I present this to you as your commission. Anytime you sense that astral projection is showing up, you have permission to, without my knowledge, cut the silver cord immediately. If you see it, you cut it. I am not dealing with this. I am not putting up with this. I am not inviting it. I am not desiring it. It is against my will that it shows up. If it shows up, you may cut it.

Thank you for being on guard for me for this. I commission you to do this in time and out of time, in Jesus' name.

We had a situation where someone astral projected to us whose link to us was the property that I lived on due to some old Freemason oaths.

Asking Heaven what we needed for the property, we were told we needed curtains and shields. We were also instructed to release the lightning of God and to release the righteousness of God.

We requested shields and curtains to be erected all about the property. We also released righteousness to the geography of the land.

We should commission our angels
to erect shields and curtains.

Father, I commission Ezekiel, his commanders and ranks to erect shields around my home and to erect curtains around my property.

I release righteousness into the geography of the land at my home. I do this in time and out of time, in the name of Jesus.

Cleansing the Land

Having asked for the shield and curtains for the land, we asked, "Is there a cleansing related to the land here that is necessary?"

We were made to understand that the land in the region where we were was not receiving the fullness of the blessing, and the geographical soil was not responding to the fullness of the blessing because of iniquity on the land in the region.

In this situation, the Ku Klux Klan had been active in the area in days past. I even recall in 5th grade seeing an image in my history book of a lynching of a black man that occurred a few miles from where I am sitting right now.

We saw in the spirit a Ku Klux Klan figure wearing a white robe and white pointed hat and were told that their activities had defiled the land. If land is defiled, a Klan member, anywhere in the region, will have freedom to do what they are doing. That freedom is like a measure of power to continue to operate. So, when we cleanse the land. We ask for an injunction and a restraining order for cleansing the land. The cleansing will be angels' work.

In this situation we were instructed to go to the Court of Land Appeals to deal with bondage on the land and those operating intentionally in deceit.

Father, we ask permission in the name of Jesus to enter the Court of Land Appeals. I would like the council of this court to help me, as I petition the court for an overturning of false verdicts on the region.

I refer to this in which Ron Horner has been moved by the hand of God, to the Pinehurst, North Carolina area, the Raleigh-Durham area and the coastline of North Carolina.

I petition this court for the overturning of a false verdict that allows demons and those operating in league with demons to use the land as a geographical pathway for unrighteousness and evil.

I am asking for a cessation of these activities by the verdict of this court.

My repentance before the court is that I repent for those who have willfully operated in deceit, willfully hiding their activities, willfully hiding slavery, willfully in rebellion against God, willfully hiding their rebellion against God, pretending that it is something else.

I repent and confess these things as sin on behalf of the humanity in this region, in the name of Jesus.

I repent for slavery of all types, gender, skin color, religious slavery, and socio-economic class slavery. Slavery of all types is a sin against a holy God. I repent on behalf of the slavery in this region. I ask you to forgive humanity involved in this, in the name of Jesus. I ask Jesus for your blood to cover these grievous sins. I choose as a son of God in the name of Jesus to forgive them, I bless them, and I release them.

I ask as an amendment to this court, for the cleansing of the land from defilement of slavery and of deceit.

I ask that the land would breathe again. I ask that the land would live again.

I ask that the land would be watered again.

I ask that the land would be connected to its source Elohim, the Creator.

I ask that the land would again be connected to its light frequency and that it would return to vibration in accordance with Heaven and the Kingdom of God.

I repent on behalf of those in the family of God who have ignored the crying out of the land.

I repent on behalf of my sisters and brothers in Jesus who have not known what to do, who have been darkened, who have withdrawn in fear from this activity, who have been blinded to it or have covered their eyes and allowed it to continue.

I repent on their behalf, in the name of Jesus, and I ask You, Father, to forgive them. I bless them, forgive them, and release them—they know not what they do. For those who do know what they do, I forgive them, too.

As an amendment to this court case. I also request that every geographical pathway being used by those operating in league with evil, be closed, shut, and locked to them; that all access to those pathways be denied to them, in the name of Jesus. I request that angels be assigned to cleanse, repair, and guard and maintain these pathways for Kingdom use.

I ask that as an amendment to this court case that all illegally obtained maps to geographical terrestrial areas that have been stolen, plundered, or obtained illegally through unrighteous trade and other means, that the maps would be destroyed, and that the land would be repossessed.

I repent for the ungodly trading of humanity that allowed Satan to have access to these maps. I confess it as sin and I ask You to forgive it by the blood of Jesus, Father. I forgive them. I bless them, and I release them.

I receive the counsel of the court and I request the injunction based on the righteous family of God that lives at _____, Pinehurst, North Carolina.

We awaited the verdict and received the agreement of the Court for the Cancellation of illegally obtained maps. We have received a verdict for the land to breathe again, and concerning the terrestrial pathways that were now being locked against evil.

The court commended us that we brought a case for the overturning of unrighteousness on the land, and we were seeking injunctions for the cleansing of the land. The court commended us for heartfelt repentance.

We did not need to request a restraining order because we had effectively obtained a restraining order, not in so many words, but as a result of the court case.

With that the court work was complete regarding the cleansing of the land (at least for this phase of it). We will continue this work as led by Heaven to do so.

Summary

- Intruders are defeated foes.
- Victory over all intruders was assured as a result of the resurrection of Jesus Christ.
- Commission our angels to take care of any intruders.
- Don't tolerate astral projection.
- Utilize curtains and shields.
- Release the lightning of God.
- Release the righteousness of God.

- Concerning land cleansing:
    - Request shields and curtains to be erected all about the property.
    - Also release righteousness to the geography of the land.
- The geographical earth soil cannot respond to the fullness of the blessing because of iniquity on the land in the region,
- Utilize the Court of Land Appeals to deal with slavery and other iniquities stored on the land and those operating intentionally and deceit.

Chapter 8

Building a Defense Against Lies

In this encounter with Heaven, Ezekiel appeared with a shepherd's staff in his hands. He explained that a shepherd's staff is a symbol of authority. Shepherds' staffs are to protect the sheep, they are not to hurt the sheep. Our willingness to engage the Father's heart for ministry is appealing to the sheep, so the Father gave the shepherd's staff to Ezekiel as a sign to us of our call to shepherd the flock, nurture them, and assist them with being the best that they are meant to be.

There is a richness in the oil of the wool of a sheep. That richness is what God is drawing out of His people. He is drawing out much richness from their realms, from their being, their calling, their books, and their destiny. The Lord is mining the riches of His Own Glory within those that He has placed on the planet in this hour. Yet those ones that He is pulling the riches of His Glory from, they need their flock, they need their tribe—their clan. They are hungry and thirsty for His goodness and His kindness. They need the association that will esteem them and think well of them.

We are being poured out as the ministry of helps[14] to those who will respond to the shepherd's staff that we have been given as an authority to shepherd a flock and rely on the free-flowing manner that Holy Spirit will cause some to enter the flock and enjoy what we are pouring out. If we are willing to enjoy them in the flock[15] when they are with us and bless them as they mingle with other flocks—this is the desire of the shepherd, the Great Shepherd, and His heart for the poor.

We are releasing revelatory flow that protects the sheep in the Fathers' flock and brings healing to the multi-dimensional beings they are. We are teaching the sheep to fly with wings they did not realize they had. This would be the spiritual access to heavenly realms that we encourage the people of God to access. This a definition of expansion.

There is a wealth of perception coming to the Bride of Christ. As we mature, a wealth of supernatural perception is coming. We must learn how to steward it. We must learn how to operate in it. We must learn what it is for and what it is not for. We must learn how to harvest it and how to sow in it. We must learn how to reap in it and how to do this with a finesse that we can

---

[14] Typically, the Greek word in this passage in 1 Corinthians 12:28-29, *antilēmpsis* is rendered "helps" although it is "laying hold of revelation or apprehending revelation, which is our particular ministry calling to the Body of Christ. (Simmons)
[15] Join us each Sunday at SandhillsEcclesia.com.

be trained in. Our job was to receive the shepherd's staff from Ezekiel as a gift from the Father.

The Lies of Crazy?

Ezekiel, as he sometimes does, will speak a word to us and then let us attempt to figure out what he is referring to. This time the word was "crazy." He asked, "What is a definition of crazy?"

We really did not know where he was going with this train of thought, so we decided that a definition of crazy is 'illogical.' He expounded further, "You have a saying where you say something is 'upside down.' The Scripture says men called good evil and evil good."[16]

"That's crazy!" he said.

We came to understand the following things. This has to do with the fact that we are living, not only in chaotic times, but we are living in crazy times and must be guarded against the lies of crazy by the hands of the angelic hosts. **For when men preach the lies as truth and do so at length, even those who know the truth run the risk of faltering in their journey and may pick up a lie instead of remaining aligned with truth.**

Therefore, angels are needed to assist us in the hour our world is in so that our lenses of truth stay on our face

---

[16] Isaiah 5:20 "Woe to those who call evil good, and good evil: who put darkness for light and light for darkness, who put bitter for sweet, and sweet for bitter!"

and our ears become stopped against lies. This is needed so that our heart resonates with truth and does not bow or be captured by the amount (meaning the quantity) of lies being taught as truth.

> *Our association and oneness with the Spirit of God is going to be the defining divider, like a very sharp sword or a surgeon's scalpel, between lies and truth.*

> *Commission our angels for the use of Truth Defender.*

Truth Defender

We began seeing what could only be described as a clear membrane stretched between door posts. If we did not know it was there, we would run into it. It was not like fabric—just a membrane. It is not really alive, but it had characteristics making us think that it was alive.

Truth Defender is a protection bubble of truth. Lies cannot penetrate it. It works through sound frequencies. Our view of it as a flesh type membrane was confirmed, but it was not made of flesh, though similar. This Truth Defender is a spiritual membrane, and it is for our protection

> *We can ask angels*
> *to bring it to our gates.*

It assists us.

If the world system and Satan are releasing lies, we are constantly having to discern between truth and lies. The amount of lies that comes bombarding us begins to weary us if we have not used discernment like muscles to consistently operate to discern.

Angels are released to help us with this need that we did not even know of. The enemy comes to vex us, and he will vex us with thoughts that are not ours, projections of lies, projections of his kingdom. We are constantly discerning to navigate between truth and lies. When we are working with Holy Spirit, receiving His wisdom, knowledge, and counsel in our ears, we are receiving all that in our gates. But there is a weapon that angels can establish at our gates that is going to *help us not feel the wearisome burden of constantly having to navigate this* because...

> *The spiritual membrane itself*
> *deflects the lies so they do not enter.*
> *Then we do not have to*
> *get rid of them.*

The reason I am presenting it like this is because the quantity or volume of lies released from world systems right now is so great that *we need a little more assistance.*

We need help from angels in our spirit gate, eye gate, ear gate—all our gates. We are going to need protection and angels have been released with these new membranes to help us. It is called Truth Defender.

We were not hearing Heaven use the word shield. Heaven did not use the word shield, although it acts like a shield. We were hearing the word *membrane* as if it was a living thing. It was a sort of covering.

Remember, we are talking about helping nurture those who belong to the Good Shepherd? And He would have me, as an under-shepherd, to shepherd those that He has brought into my flock by helping them receive what is useful to them, what is beneficial to them. So, by releasing the understanding of a truth covering, inviting angels to bring the Membrane of Truth Covering to my gate this will assist those who may have a harder time in their struggle to discern truth and lies.

The Banner of Truth

In the spirit realm, a banner marks those who belong to Jesus. It is a marker or a distinguisher of those who belong to Jesus—those who are under His covering and under His protection. It is as if the Father has extended this garment to the Son, and Jesus willingly spreads it over His people like one would spread a blanket over a child or spread it over an animal. A person would put this lovingly over them. It is not a tent. It is not a shield. It is not a curtain. It is kind of like a garment, but it is much more. It feels like a membrane. It assists us because there are some things we just do not need to be worried about. There are some lies that just need to fall to the ground. It is the assistance of the Father to give this to us.

A lot is going on in the spirit that is directed to cause a diverting and distracting of the people of God. They just need some help. It will help by causing the fiery darts of lies and the cold, steel-black smog of lies from penetrating our realms. **We are going to do this by requesting the angels to bring the covering of Truth Defender and establish Truth Defender at our gates.**

Commission angels to see to it that the chaotic craziness that is in the world does not penetrate our realm.

We are going to be clearer for it. We are going to have abilities of our spirit, as well as our heart, and our mind. Even our flesh will respond well to this protection that has been afforded to us.

I thank You, Father. Thank you, Holy Spirit. Thank you, Jesus, for this gift. I readily receive the Membrane of Truth Defender on my behalf.

This Truth Defender is something a person can be under or behind because we can look at it two ways: behind it or under it. It is so powerful in the spirit that it is going to help the people of God be who they are amid the bombardment of crazy as we yield to what Heaven is telling us about this in *this* time (because we are going to need it in future time events).

Commission angels to use the Truth Defender Membrane.

I request of the Father the Membrane of Truth Defender.

I call my angels near, in the name of Jesus. [Wait until you sense their arrival before proceeding.]

I commission you to establish this needed Membrane of Truth Defender at my gates—the gates of my spirit, the gates of my body, and the gates of my soul.

Establish the Membrane of Truth Defender in the gates of the spheres of my influence, the gates of the extension of my boundary lines to the point we are moving in, and to the point we are moving into—to our next expansion.

I commission you to do all this in time and out of time.

[By the way, we must think very multidimensionally about this with truth.]

I welcome the Banner of Truth Defender over God's people—over those who have drawn near to this ministry outlet—this flock of the Great

Shepherd—this family of God—this tribe of His beloved.

I commission you for the establishment of the Membrane of Truth Defender on every dimensional access point and gateway.

I thank You, Father for the angel Ezekiel, his commanders, and ranks being commissioned to assist other angels in the establishment of this Truth Defender Banner.

I commission my angels to work with Ezekiel, his commanders, and ranks in the establishment of this Truth Defender Banner in my realms as well and at my gateways.

I thank You, Father, for such a rich gift as this. I thank You, for Your benefits are never-ending. Your care for Your people and for Your Glory in Your people, You are jealous for that, and I thank You for that.

Thank You, Father, for the continual infilling of Your people with the Spirit of Truth and how You are making your people discerners of truth, discerners of revelation knowledge without mixture. We praise You for that.

Assaulted Emotions

One of the reasons we need the Truth Defender Banner (which is a membrane and a covering over our soul realm) is because the enemy will use emotions against God's people. He will infiltrate emotions with lies.

> *The Membrane of Truth Defender is needed at the gateway of our emotions.*

It is *also needed* at the gateway of our heart, for with our heart we choose a thing—we choose a path, and we decide to walk in it.

We may also discern that we need this Truth Defender covering over our heart gateways as well. Here is a commissioning:

I commission my angels to work with the Truth Defender Banner and to establish it over my heart pathways and gates, in time and out of time, in Jesus' name.

As we completed that commissioning, we heard the sound of drums. It was explained to us that they were warfare drums. The establishment of the Truth Defender Banner is a declaration of the Kingdom that we are in and are serving. It is an 'in your face' type of positioning against the enemy. It is a declaration of war, but it is really a declaration of victory. The drums were announcing that.

We thank You, Father for the richness of this gift, that angels would bring the Truth Defender Banner and covering to Your people in this hour. Thank You, Father, for the impenetrable nature of it to the lies of the enemy.

Acceptance in the Father's Kingdom

One thing that will help us with this new understanding that Ezekiel brought to us and has assisted us with understanding is the word 'acceptance' in the Father's Kingdom. There are things to accept because our mind is not capable of categorizing—some things in the earth plane, but *the acceptance of the benefit* of them *is* what we are capable of. 'Do we accept?' is a similar question to 'Do we receive?' but *receive is the initial taking hold of* and *accept is the standing within*. Do we accept to stand within the gift of the weapon that Ezekiel has brought to our understanding?

We do! We accept it. Not just from Ezekiel, but from our Father, from our Father's Kingdom, and from the King Himself.

This is going to be helpful, because we have not even realized how often God's people are doing the work of the discerning. They are doing the work of the sifting of the lies from the truth in their world, in their understanding of who they are, in their understanding of who other people are, in their understanding of what God wants to do in the earth realm. They are even sifting through the understanding of what the earth is and is not, and what the earth can be and can do. As we know, we are constantly doing that. There is a frequency vibration that we are not aware of, that in the overuse of that is actually *not rest*. This is an attempt to help God's people be more at rest in Him, because this is now a defense against the crazy, chaotic, and upside down.

Utilizing Our Bandwidth

The defeated foe operates in chaos.
His realm is chaos.

There is no order. Therefore, he is a child of wrath. This is why he has deep corruption in his being.

Think of it like this. If some of our bandwidth is always being utilized for the defense of the truth, and is always in the midst of the working out of the discerning of truth, would that take away from other things we are meant to be doing with that bandwidth? The defense of this by the hands of angels comes through the establishment of Truth Defender as a covering. It operates to deflect lies **before** they penetrate the realm, the place where we must decide about the lies or discern about the lies, in regard to the heart.

With Truth Defender in place, we have the wherewithal to receive the flow of revelation easier from the Father because we are not having to fight second realm heavens or earth realm distractions like that.

The Bench of Rest

There is a bench of rest where we can sit down and rest. And not only rest, but from the position of rest, laugh at the enemies' antics because of his corruption that he brought on himself. It is like sitting on a park bench with Jesus watching the crazy go by, knowing it cannot touch us, and we do not have to worry about it. It also causes the frequency in our being to be more at rest. We need that.

Maximizing Bandwidth

A few days later I engaged Heaven about what we had heard. Heaven shared more about bandwidth with me. The message about bandwidth is a good one to recognize. The question is, 'How much bandwidth is left for the Fathers' purposes after the soul gets done filling itself with information that is sometimes of no permanent merit? (Attention news junkies!)

Always reserve the majority of bandwidth for our spirit to operate from.

> *It is the conduit to Heaven
> and heavenly things.*

We want that bandwidth maximized. We want the flow of Heaven maximized.

With Truth Defender Membrane in place, we can learn to maximize bandwidth by praying in the spirit. It keeps a constant bandwidth with Heaven and the heavenly realm. It bypasses the intellect—hence, the soul—to keep the connection with Heaven. It has not been understood for the strength and benefit it carries for our spirit man and its overall well-being. The choice to speak in tongues with strength only *works to strengthen the work* that is accomplished by praying in the spirit continuously.

> *Praying in the spirit keeps
> a constant bandwidth with Heaven
> and the heavenly realm.*

I challenge us to instruct our spirit to pray in the spirit continuously. Try it and report back the difference. Then take up a challenge to 5-minute stints of speaking in tongues aloud non-stop, increasing that in regular intervals. It will activate many things in our behalf.

> *Praying in the spirit aligns our times.*

One of the works praying in the spirit does is to **align our times**. We have appointments on our calendar with Heaven that need the fine tuning and the adjustments of Heaven to *coordinate the angelic intersections that maximize these appointments.* Some are more finely tuned to the workings of their calendar than others, but all need to be more finely attuned.

The day of Pentecost occurred at a precise moment in time. Those waiting in the upper room were not waiting so much to get spiritually attuned (which they *were* doing), but they were waiting for the precise *kairos* to occur. When the clock hit the top of the hour on that day, Heaven released in a flood, and it was magnificent. Hell was not expecting that to occur. Hell was set on its heels by the events of that day.

> *Hell cannot control what it does not know is coming.*

Speaking in tongues *helps facilitate hell's ignorance,* for it bypasses typical channels that hell has learned to inject itself into and interfere. However, *this channel is off limits to Satan and his forces*—wherever they are—in whatever realm, dimension, space in time, etc. He has been fully defeated in this manner. Rejoice in the victory that we get to *participate in* **and** *reinforce* every time we pray in the spirit or speak in tongues.

My engagement with Heaven was then over, and I had gained more understanding in several arenas. Here are two versions of a commissioning for our angels concerning the Membrane of Truth Defender:

Commissionings for Our Angels

Short Version

I call the angels assigned to me to come near. [Wait until you sense their nearness. Once you sense their arrival, verbally say:]

I commission my angels to work with the Truth Defender Banner and to establish it over my heart pathways and gates, in Jesus' name.

I commission you to these things in time and out of time, in Jesus' name.

Extended Version

I call the angels assigned to me to come near.

[Await the sense of their arrival. Once you sense their arrival, verbally say:]

I commission you to establish the Membrane of Truth Defender at my gates—the gates of my spirit, the gates of my body, and the gates of my soul.

Establish the Membrane of Truth Defender in the gates of the spheres of my influence, the gates at the extension of my boundary lines to the point I am moving in, and to the point I am moving into— to my next expansion.

I welcome the Banner of Truth Defender over me.

I commission you for the establishment of the Membrane of Truth Defender at every dimensional access point and gateway.

I thank You, Father, for the angel Ezekiel, his commanders, and ranks being commissioned to assist other angels in the establishment of this Truth Defender Banner.

I commission my angels to work with Ezekiel, his commanders, and ranks in the establishment of this Truth Defender Banner in my realms and at my gateways.

I commission my angels to work with the Truth Defender Banner and to establish it over my heart pathways and gates, and to do all this in time and out of time, in Jesus' name.

I thank You, Father, for this rich gift.

Thank You, Father, for continually infilling me with the Spirit of Truth and that You are making me a discerner of truth and a discerner of revelation knowledge without mixture. I praise You for that, in Jesus' name.

Summary

- Heaven is releasing revelatory flow that protects the sheep in the Fathers' flock and brings healing to the multi-dimensional beings they are.
- Heaven is teaching the sheep to fly with wings they did not realize they had.
- There is a wealth of perception coming to the Bride of Christ as we mature.
- We must learn how to steward it.
- We must learn how to operate in it.
- We must learn what it is for and what it is not for.
- We must learn how to harvest it and how to sow in it.
- We must learn how to reap in it and how to do this with a finesse that we can be trained in.
- We are living not *only* in chaotic times, but we are living in crazy times.
- We must be guarded against the lies of crazy by the hands of the angelic hosts.
- When men preach the lies as truth and do so at length, even those who know the truth run the risk of faltering in their journey and may pick up a lie, instead of remaining aligned with truth.
- Angels are needed to assist us in the hour in which our world is in so that
    - Our lenses of truth stay on our face
    - Our ears become stopped against lies

- Our heart resonates with truth and does not bow or be captured by the quantity of lies being taught as truth.
- Our association and oneness with the Spirit of God is going to be the defining divider, like a very sharp sword or a surgeon's scalpel, between lies and truth.
- We will need to commission angels for the Truth Defender.
- Truth Defender is a protection bubble of truth.
    - Lies cannot penetrate it.
    - It works through sound frequencies.
    - We can ask angels to bring it to our gates.
- The spiritual membrane itself deflects the lies so they do not enter.
    - Then we do not have to get rid of them.
- The Banner of Truth feels like a marker or a distinguisher of
    - Those who belong to Jesus
    - Those who are under His covering
    - Those who are under His protection.
- It is going to help by causing the fiery darts of lies and the cold, steel-black smog of lies from penetrating our realms.
- We are going to do this by requesting the angels to bring the covering of Truth Defender and
- Establish Truth Defender at our gates.

- Commission angels to see that the chaotic craziness that is in the world does not penetrate our realm.
- The Membrane of Truth Defender is also needed at the gateway of our heart
- Often God's people are doing the work of the discerning.
- They are doing the work of the sifting of the lies of the truth in their world:
    - In their understanding of who they are,
    - In their understanding of who other people are,
    - In their understanding of what God wants to do in the earth realm,
    - In the understanding of what the earth is and is not, and
    - What the earth can be and can do.
- Truth Defender is a covering.
- Know how it operates to deflect lies before they penetrate the realm where we must decide about them or discern about them.
- With Truth Defender in place, we have the wherewithal to receive the flow of revelation easier from the Father because we are not having to fight second realm heavens or earth realm distractions.
- Praying in the spirit keeps a constant bandwidth with Heaven and the heavenly realm.

- It bypasses the intellect—hence, the soul—to keep the connection with Heaven.
- Challenge the people—the flock—to instruct their spirit to pray in the spirit continuously.
- One of the works praying in the spirit does is to align our times.
- Hell cannot control what it does not know is coming.

Chapter 9
Obtaining Clarity & Balance

When we engaged Heaven on this Wednesday morning, Ezekiel appeared. We could see scales of justice (like we use on our logo). Ezekiel began sharing about balance. We learned several things in this engagement.

Many things are in the balance, and they are being balanced and measured for judgment. The righteous ones of God will be found true.

If we are seeking the King and His Kingdom, we have nothing to be concerned about.

A balancing in nations is taking place. Patience will be needed for this journey for various times and events.

The breastplate of righteousness must be securely fastened. The times ahead require us to rest in His righteousness as He performs a roll call of judgments. It is time for shades and veils that have covered things to be coming off.

The student of the Spirit of God will agree to be taught and stand in a willingness to surrender preconceived thinking and expectations. Another view of the balance that God's people need is to look to their smaller spheres of influence—their families and friends—and balance this with what they partake of as a larger movement of humanity. Yet we must never cease to cry out to the Lord that His righteous works, His will—the will of God, **be done** on earth—not the works of His people, but of Him directly.

Notice I say the righteous works of the King, the Lord Jesus. Not the righteous works of His people; for a balance exists of this where the people of God cry out to God for His works of righteousness.

This is a time for the crying out for His works of righteousness.

What Ezekiel was showing us was the balance between not becoming out of balance, where we are just consumed with our little sphere of what's going on in *our* world, but we also have eyes to understand the larger sphere of the planet and to cry out to the Father for His righteous works. There is a connection to that where the righteous works of God would be made manifest in the earth. These are the timed events of Heaven as Heaven does what Heaven does.

But it is because His people have cried out to Him, as they cried out from their slavery to Pharoah. They cry out to God, and these cries arise.

We were instructed to remind our audience to **put fear far from them**. This era is not a time for the people of God to fail in their view of fear, but to remain in faith that God is good. That He has assigned His assignments.

We must remain staunchly unafraid of our future in God, so that the faithfulness of God can fulfill its purpose in our life.

The Substance of Clarity

We then asked Ezekiel what he was in need of, and he requested Angel Elixir, Angel Food, and Angel Bread, as well as shields.

He began to talk to us about a substance. He recently talked to us about Fog Dispeller. There is another substance called Clarity. It is like Windex®[17] we would use to clean a mirror. It is a substance of Heaven that angels use that brings clarity. It clarifies details so they can be seen, and nuances observed. It provides definition. When we look in a camera with a zoom lens,

---

[17] Windex® is a liquid glass cleaner.

and we zoom in and zoom out, we are looking for a definition of the tiny things.

Arm angels with Clarity—
the substance of Clarity.

We are going to need to see ourselves reflected with the substance of clarity. And we are going to need to see that events are reflected through Clarity to bring definition, to bring the fine details out, to be able to see the fine grain, the finer details.

For the angel Ezekiel, his commanders, and ranks, we request that they be supplied with Angel Elixir, Angel Food, Angel Bread, and shields. I request they be supplied with the Substance of Clarity.

I commission you, Ezekiel, to use the Substance of Clarity on our behalf and in our realms, that we may see with finer definition. I commission you to the use of the shields on behalf of the people of God for their protection.

I commission you to these things, in time and out of time, in Jesus' name.

The Substance of Clarity is also for our protection against what we call sound waves—the bombardment of evil plots and schemes. May the lies of the enemy fall to the ground.

I commission you, Ezekiel, to establish these shields around us, around the staff, around those who have sown into this ministry, around those who are seeking God with the assistance of the revelation that we provide. We ask for these shields to be erected for the purpose so that evil sound does not penetrate the realms of God's people aligned with us due to your actions.

I commission you to these things, in time and out of time, in Jesus' name.

We can use the Substance of Clarity when a fog bank or a blanket is trying to be put over a business which has sound vibrations in it that are saying complete and utter falsehoods like, "There is a shortage. There is not enough, there is never going to be enough, we cannot do this, we cannot do that. This will not work. That needs to change." It is a fog bank of complete falsehoods. The Substance of Clarity will enable us to see the opposite of what is coming from the fog bank. It is rather amazing because *there IS enough! There is ALWAYS plenty!* We *CAN* do it a new way! We are *going to do* it that new way!

When we start saying the truth about what we see that fog bank gets pushed back, like how fog eddies and moves and floats. But when we start releasing the truth against it, the fog makes way—it moves. It is like seeing the mountain move into the sea because we just said it, and our faith is that we are in that realm of seeing *this is not so impossible*. But *we have got to say it!*

> *We have to say what the truth is because of the amount of falsehood coming forth.*

There is the falsehood from Satan, who is rather lazy, saying, "If we can stop them by just filling the atmosphere with those falsehoods, then that's the easy way." But the way we, the saints, pierce through the falsehoods is by releasing this Substance of Clarity to angels—and to commission them to release the Clarity.

> *Commission our angels to release Clarity.*

Then **we have to begin to say what the truth is when we start seeing it.** "There *IS* plenty! There *IS* enough! The government *IS* going to align with righteousness! Things *ARE* going to be exposed! People *ARE* going to be judged and come to justice, even in a civil justice system!"

As we begin to speak this, we may see the plot of the enemy. The plot is to get people to sit down, to give up, and to let their hands hang limp by their side, so they have given up even before the battle has begun. They have given up at the first little fog bank. That's all it is—a *fog* bank.

> *We have to say the opposite of the falsehood.*

We have got to call the falsehood on the carpet. Actually, there *IS* enough! There *IS* plenty. There *IS* plenty of time. There *ARE* plenty of resources. There *ARE* plenty of personnel. There *ARE* plenty of people who want to work. Instead of repeating what evil media is projecting, we have to be the loudspeaker to *project the opposite.*

We must remember to be kind to the people, for the people are trying. The families of God are trying, but they are under such blindfolds.

The work of the enemy is to blindfold the families of God.

Another plot is saying, "Us four and no more!" It makes us circle the wagons. It makes us look into our own little pod. We cannot be doing that right now.[18]

With that our engagement was over. Now, anyone may use the following template to commission their angels with these mighty weapons of war.

Commission angels to use the mighty weapons of war.

---

[18] See blog post on familial spirits:
https://www.courtsofheavenwebinars.com/post/the-insiduous-work-of-familial-spirits

Search the blog posts on our website for more weaponry revelation we have received recently:

www.courtsofheavenwebinars.com

Commission for Our Angels

I call the angels assigned to me to come near. (Wait until we sense their nearness.)

Father, in the name of Jesus, I request they be supplied with shields and with the Substance of Clarity.

I commission you to use the Substance of Clarity on my behalf and in my realms, that I may see with finer definition.

I commission you to these things, both in time and out of time, in Jesus' name.

Summary

- The breastplate of righteousness must be securely fastened.

- The times ahead require us to rest in His righteousness as He performs a roll call of judgments.

- It is time for shades and veils that have covered things to be coming off.

- The student of the Spirit of God will agree to be taught and stand in a willingness to surrender preconceived thinking and expectations.

- This is a time for the crying out for His works of righteousness.

- Remind our audience to put fear far from them.

- This era is not a time for the people of God to fail in their view of fear, but to remain in faith that God is good.

- We must remain staunchly unafraid of our future in God so that the faithfulness of God can fulfill its purpose in our life.

- The Substance of Clarity clarifies details so they can be seen, and nuances observed. It provides definition.

- Have the people arm their angels with Clarity—the Substance of Clarity.

- We have to begin to say what the truth is when we start seeing it.

The work of the enemy is to blindfold the families of God.

Chapter 10

The Angel of the Broad Sword

This encounter was unusual in the aspect of the angel we encountered. When we inquired who he was, he declared, "I am the Angel of the Broad Sword. I am from the realms of Heaven. I have been assigned to assist your realm with the division of light and dark, false and true, evil and righteous, for the purpose of the domain of understanding within your being."

He remarked, "I am tasked with this from the Father. You did not ask for me. I was sent."

This angel was very tall. He had a very long, very tall sword that was wide. It was wide at the base, and it tapered. It looked very heavy, but he didn't act like it was heavy.

Commission to the Angel of the Broad Sword

I speak to the Angel of the Broad Sword, in the name of Jesus. I thank you for coming. I thank you for fulfilling your assignment. We are in agreement with your work.

I commission you to the full extent of your assignment in the realm of LifeSpring International Ministries, its realms, its relationships, its destiny, its purpose, its calling, and to those who are aligned as students, listeners, or purchasers, or those who have sown seed, members, purchasers of books, our audience, purchasers of courses, and those who have prayed for us, even when they do not know that they have prayed for us. I commission you to your work and thank you for making yourself available.

He is a type of gatekeeper at the gates. This is why he has a sword that divides, because we cannot pass through his gate lest we have a division of these things. But he also works on our behalf, assisting us to gain knowledge of the division. This is blessed because it is for us. It's a gift for us from the Father that we couldn't know of, and we couldn't have designed it. This one is working on our behalf from the Father and the hand of the Father.

And I also commission you, Angel of the Broad Sword, to work with Ezekiel, his commanders, and his ranks, and the network of the angels in my realms, in Jesus' name. I am in total agreement with what you have been sent to do. I thank the Father for your coming. I commission you to these things both in time and out of time, in Jesus' name.

We can recognize his work through our knowledge of clarity, of vision, our extended vision, our understanding of Heaven and heavenly beings, our acceptance of the grace for our time, and the knowledge that we are not without resources. He continues shedding abroad the light of His glory.

This angel was also pretty mysterious and awe inspiring. When he planted the sword tip down, it was what we think of might divide a tectonic plate. It would divide it asunder. It was to pry things apart. He said, "I will tell you this has something to do with the mind. Trust in my work."

I had the question, "Is there an angel that does that division, the Hebrews 4:12 soul and spirit division?"

We decided to ask Lydia for insight.

Dividing Truth from Untruth

We asked permission to speak to Lydia in the business complex, and once she appeared, we explained to her, "We met someone new sent by the Father—the Angel of the Broad Sword. "

Lydia asked, "What did he tell you?"

We explained that he was sent by the Father and that he works on our behalf, dividing things.

She said, "Yes, that's dividing truth and untruth, dividing and parting, that you and those who align with LifeSpring, as those who agree may have greater dimensions of division of truth versus untruth. I would add that he works in the background, and you are blessed to receive that. You may see the dividing between illusion and disillusion, the false from the truth, by the Lamp of the Lord within—the Holy Spirit's lamp within you. I rejoice that the Father has sent him to the ministry."

His type of rank is assigned. His work in his angelic realm is the warfare of the division between these things, not within the division of the person, but in the division of the realm.

Think of your student's work. They are engaged with court cases to free themselves from the bondage of being one with evil, having partaken of or having become one with evil—like eating food. When we eat food, we become that food. Right? So, historically in the bloodline, we have those who have eaten spiritual food and become partakers with evil. These things have to be divided out, but they are divided out in different dimensional things, not just our being's realm—our body, soul, or spirit realm, but in realms of dimensions. His work is to do dimensional work. Anywhere there is a hunger for the knowledge of the difference of those things, his work is in that realm. We would link to that. This Angel of the Broad Sword is assigned to us by the Father for the work that we are doing in bringing this before others.

We asked, "Is there a commission that we need to do with him?"

She replied, "Did you agree with him?"

We replied that we did.

Lydia continued, "It would not be a commissioning, like you would commission Ezekiel. His work is of a different magnitude. **He gets his commission from the Father.**"

So, we agreed with his work for the Father and spoke it aloud. That is why he made himself known, so that we would agree with this work because it's a co-laboring—a co-partnering.

We sensed a majesty about him, and Lydia explained the reason for that was because of the rank that he is from and His work to reveal the glory of God. It is majestic and a majestic thing he does.

Summary

- The Angel of the Broadsword is a type of gatekeeper at the gates.
- He also works on our behalf, assisting us to gain knowledge of division.
- We can recognize his work by:
    - Our knowledge of clarity,

- Vision,
- Our extended vision,
- Our understanding of Heaven and heavenly beings,
- Our acceptance of the grace for our time, and
- The knowledge that we are not without resources.
- He was sent by the Father.
- He works on our behalf of dividing things.
    - Dividing truth and untruth,
    - Those who align with LifeSpring may have greater dimensions of division of truth versus untruth.
- He works in the background.
- We may see the dividing between:
    - Illusion and disillusion,
    - The false from the truth, by the Lamp of the Lord within—the Holy Spirit's Lamp within us.
- His work in his angelic realm is the warfare of the division between these things.
- He gets his commission from the Father.

Chapter 11
Angelic Engagement

Ezekiel began a sidenote saying, "There are some reading your books, and when they read about me, they are trying to engage me. It would be good for you to talk with them about their need to engage their *own* angels, the angels assigned to them as their personal angel, but *also other angels assigned to them*. There are other angels assigned to them, too. Not all angels are going to have a relationship with them in that they talk to them, but use the phrase 'the angels assigned to me.'"

When we speak of or to Ezekiel, it is because he is the angel of *this* ministry. Some, as they read the books, are trying to engage with Ezekiel at the level we are engaging with him. This is inappropriate.

Just remember, there is an order of angels. All things in the angelic world are ordered. I'm being very plain. It is not appreciated when things are out of order or places tried to be entered that are outside of one's authorization.

We should primarily follow the leading of the Spirit of God within us. Receive teaching from the Spirit of God. Receive direction, leading, and prompting from the Spirit of God. We can ask Holy Spirit to show us our angels. Many are operating immaturely in this, where they are trying *from their soul realm* to make connection to an angel. This is not how it works.

Our human spirit and Holy Spirit oneness connect us with the realm of angelic activity.

Do not be impatient to meet an angel. *Nor should we agree with the enemy* that our angel is not present. Many angels are present, and backup angels are always present. Do not fall to the lie of the enemy that he has captured more angels than have been captured. This is false. We must be discerning in our spirit, with the help of Holy Spirit, the author of discernment. If we believe our angel to be captured, when our angel is *not* captured, this hurts our angel. It causes a warfare in that angels' realm. We must believe what Holy Spirit is showing us about our angel.

A plot is afoot against the sons and daughters of God who are learning about angels, to make them think their angel isn't present or is captured.

Do not make assumptions from our soul and intellect, but be surrendered to the Holy Spirit's truth. This is a ploy to bring warfare in the angelic realm. Resist this. There are many contributions to why we have things taking place in our realms that have nothing to do with our angel. Be discerning. Seek Holy Spirit and the Kingdom of God. Ask for help at the Help Desk. Do not fall to the lie of the enemy from our soul realm telling us that our angel is missing. Every angel who is missing is noted in Heaven, and the battle is working itself out for the rescue of these angels. Occasionally, we will see an angel missing, but this is not the norm. The enemy is plotting to make us think that it is so, so that he has greater inroad into the battle—the skirmish.

Our belief, as we grow in these things and mature in these things, is very necessary. We must believe in our angel.

Having faith that angels have been assigned to us increases the ability of our angels.

We are linked that way, and remember there *are* enough angels.

Summary

- We must learn to engage our own angels including:

- the angels assigned to us as our personal angel, but also
  - other angels assigned to us.
- It is not appreciated when things are out of order or places tried to be entered that are outside of ones' authorization.
- Ask Holy Spirit to show us our angels.
- Many are operating immaturely in this, where they are trying from their soul realm to make connection to an angel.
- Our human spirit and Holy Spirit oneness connect us with the realm of angelic activity.
- Many angels are present, and backup angels are always present.
- Do not fall to the lie of the enemy that he has captured more angels than have been captured.
- There are many contributions to why we have things taking place in our realm that have nothing to do with our angel.
- Be discerning. Seek Holy Spirit and the Kingdom of God.
- Ask for help at the Help Desk.
- We must believe in our angel.
- Having faith that angels have been assigned to us increases the ability of our angels.

Chapter 12

Calendar Seeds

We had engaged Heaven concerning the "when" for an upcoming meeting that was in the early planning stages. Once we had worked out a few details, Lydia (the woman in white assigned to our ministry) began to share about speaking in faith over our calendar. She said, "Speak faith *to* your calendar."

Our calendar is a living being. When accessing the Business Complex to view our business or ministry calendar, we need to understand that it is not a static, dead thing, but rather it is a living being.

I described it as the characters in the animated Disney movie, *The Beauty and the Beast* where the teapot and the candlestick were alive and moving. It appears similar to that only and not necessarily in an animated fashion. Because it is living we can interact with it.

Word Seeding

When we discuss our calendar, we must release faith-filled words over it. We must 'word-seed' it. Some of the seeds will take off and begin to grow. Those are the ones we will cultivate. We discuss potential dates for an upcoming meeting, and we word-seed those dates. They begin to grow. From the optional dates, one will look more promising. We will begin to see this in our calendar. What begins to grow? What begins to take root? Wouldn't we cultivate the seedling that looks the healthiest? Whereas one seedling did not take root, or it did not get as much root as the others based on the words spoken over them.

As we continue to discuss this with those involved in the process, we will see the word related to when it begins to grow. It will take on more vigor. That would be the one to go to. It's done by bathing a word-seed with faith. The impression of Holy Spirit will bring our mind to a conclusion as well, like we knew to wait and not make any plans until we heard something.

Commission Concerning Our Calendar

I call the angels assigned to me to come near. (Wait until you sense their nearness.)

I commission you to the full outworking of my calendar. Cause the appointments assigned by Heaven to be fulfilled completely.

Cause those appointments that would be of little or no value to be cancelled and not waste my time.

I commission you to work with the angels of the other parties involved in my calendar to bring all the parties together at the right time to accomplish the purposes Heaven has designed for that moment in time.

I commission you to cause the intersection of the miracles of Heaven regarding my time and my calendar.

I commission you to protect my calendar from intrusions, interferences, time-wasters, and items of no value.

Cause my calendar to be filled according to the books of Heaven for my life, in Jesus' name.

I commission the angels assigned to me to all these things, in time and out of time, in Jesus' name.

Summary

- Learn to speak faith to our calendar.
- Our calendar is not a static, dead thing, but rather it is a living being.
- When we discuss our calendar we release faith-filled words over it.
- We "word-seed" our calendar

- Some of the seeds will take off and begin to grow
- Those are the ones we will cultivate
- Learn to bathe a word-seed with faith
- The impression of Holy Spirit will bring our mind to a conclusion.

Chapter 13
The Angel of Inventory

Adina and I had just moved into a new home and the following morning after the move, I heard these instructions in my journaling time:

> *Remember to call upon the Angel of Inventory. He knows where everything was placed—EVERYTHING. Acquaint yourself with him and his function. Just like other things in Heaven, Heaven has lists of everything that you packed and where it was placed. Heaven does this for every believer.*
>
> *To know where things seemingly disappeared to is helpful and helps to alleviate stress that can occur when you cannot recall where something was packed. He can highlight the box, give an image of the item being placed in a box or other container, and even provide you with an inventory list of each container. It is not hard for Heaven to provide these things to the sons and daughters, as the Father wants His sons and*

daughters to be able to rest in their journey. Remember, John wrote, 'In my Father's house are many roadside stations' (ARTB).[19] These are resting places on a journey just as you used to see on the roadways of your nation where picnic tables were provided for enjoyment and to provide a resting place. Then you had the small motels and cabins that provided a place for overnight lodging. The Father is all about rest and not about stress or striving. He does not want that for His sons and daughters as it damages their bodies and emotional state. He wants them to live in health and wholeness. Fulness of joy is their portion.

Ask the Angel of Inventory to guide you to where the things you have need of were placed. Pay attention to the nudges you will experience, for they will often be quite gentle. It is a co-laboring with the angels that Father is building with His sons and daughters, and you get to participate in it.

The final part of that, is if you are having trouble receiving the information, access a seer and the seer gift. They can help.

---

[19] John 14:2

Commission for the Angel of Inventory

I call the angels assigned to me to come near, as well as the Angel of Inventory.

I commission you, in the name of Jesus, to guide me to the thing(s) I have need of. Uncover it if it needs uncovering, cover it if it needs covering. Nudge me where to look to discover this item.

I commission you to these things, in time and out of time, in Jesus' name.

Summary

- The Angel of Inventory knows where everything was placed—EVERYTHING.
- We can acquaint ourselves with him and his function.
- Heaven has lists of everything that we packed and where it was placed.
- Heaven does this for every believer as well.
- To know where things seemingly disappeared to is helpful and helps to alleviate stress that can occur when we cannot recall where something was packed. He can-
    - Highlight the box,
    - Give an image of the item being placed in a box or other container, and
    - Even provide us with an inventory list of each container.

Chapter 14

Working with Our Assignments

As we stepped into Heaven to find out what we were to talk about that evening in the Mentoring Group,[20] all kinds of musical sounds could be heard. They were happy sounds. We wanted to know what these happy sounds were and discovered that these are the joy sounds of heaven. The joy of celebration, the joy of Jesus' beauty. The joy of His success. The celebration of His courts.

The people of God need to know that they can come to Heaven to receive this sound of Heaven. They suffer because they lack seeking after the Kingdom of God. This is seeking after the Kingdom of God, when our soul is stepped back, our body is relaxed, and our spirit man is forward, ascending through Heaven to hear the heavenly sounds.

---

[20] This is a free weekly meeting. Register for the link at our website: CourtsOfHeavenWebinars.com.

The sound could be felt in our spirits before it was heard. It was very joyful. It was very lighthearted. There was not a negative thing in the sounds. What beautiful sounds of Heaven they were!

It was the sound of Heaven's fellowship. We can enjoy enjoying the presence of the Son. His presence is everywhere in Heaven. All of Heaven easily enjoys His presence. *We can come and easily enjoy His presence.* We lose out because we do not step into Heaven and hear those heavenly sounds.

Sereneness of Purpose

We suddenly were experiencing a shift to a more quiet, sober atmosphere, a sereneness of purpose. It was the subtraction of busy-ness. It was the flow of purpose. It had things to do, things to accomplish, and places to be. But it did not hold distraction, and it did not hold busy-ness. It did not hold anxiety. It did not hold anxiety about the outcome. It held faith and belief in a good outcome. This is His presence for the increase of His glory on the earth, to be at peace and operate from peace. Peace is a strength of Heaven, and we can engage this peace from our spirit– from our spirit man.

Sometimes humanity in the body of Christ is trying to do the work that angels are supposed to do, and the humans get in a state of anxiety. Angels are supposed to war on our behalf. We are supposed to direct, co-labor, and work with them. We simply must believe that they are capable.

Have No Curiosity of Darkness

When people find out about demonic entities, such as Leviathan, they begin to wonder and have some curiosity about it. They step over into alignment with Leviathan. That's not good. We can know about it, but *we need not know **everything** about it or worry about it.* We will need to just put angels to work about it. We should call our angels near and let our angels step in.

We are not meant to fight against Leviathan, so let the angels of the Host fight through the angelic network.

When Ezekiel tells us that he has been working against Leviathan in victory, the anxiety we feel is because we have overstepped into thinking we need to do something about that *when it is Ezekiel that does things about that.* We just *direct him* and *see what he needs.* We get to see what the victory is. Our job is to continue to encourage him in his activity against Leviathan.

*Remember,
Leviathan is a defeated spirit.
It is an absolutely defeated spirit.*

What humans do is they think about that wicked spirit and forget that it is defeated, so it grows.

> *The deception is that it will grow in their mind as an undefeated spirit when it is **totally** defeated.*

It knows it is defeated, but *it is counting on the fact that we forget that.* It is counting on the fact that we do not know it is defeated, and *then* it can work against us. *It works through deception.* So, we must be very discerning about it.

> *We must think of these spiritual entities that have been defeated as very small, because they **all** are small.*

But what they do is they project themselves as large, as impenetrable, as impossible. They are lying to us. They are deceiving us. We are greater than they are.[21] We are more powerful than they are because we are in Jesus.

> *We have a bigger projection than they do, because we project from the realm of the Kingdom of God.*

Yet, when we forget that and try to overcome them from our humanity—from the physical plane—then we

---

[21] 1 John 4:4

are unequally matched, but *angels are NOT unequally matched*.

> *Do not let the enemy project his largeness to us when he is little and under our feet.*

As often is the case when speaking with Lydia or Ezekiel, when they are done with a subject, all discussion has ended on that topic. The topic then changed to the subject of assignments.

Receiving Assignments

The people of God who are seeking the Kingdom are the ones who receive assignments. The people of God who have yet to learn to seek for the Kingdom of God are not receiving assignments from Heaven, instead they are making them up and *assuming that there is an assignment when there is not*. This causes the body of Christ to suffer unnecessarily and needlessly. An assignment from Heaven can be known when we seek the Kingdom. We can *step into realms of Heaven and ask* if there is an assignment for us, or *Holy Spirit can give us the unction* that we have an assignment.

Assignments are activities—sometimes of words and sometimes a deed.

> *Assignments work to bring the peace of God to the earth.*

They work to bring the manifestation of the principles of Yahweh to earth. They often have signs that follow them.

When one completes an assignment or is working through an assignment in faith, there are many signs along the way to confirm, but assignments are spiritual things. They come from Heaven. They do not come from the earth realm. They do not come from the intellect. They do not come from thinking it up.

---

*Assignments can be found
in the Court of Records.*

Saints can enter the Court of Records and find out if there is an assignment list and discover what is at the top of the list. Some saints may be surprised at what is at the top of their assignment list.

Assignments from Heaven come with timing. So, if we have missed an assignment, it may no longer be on our assignment list because the timing for that in our life has passed. Heaven knows that we are in time. Heaven knows that we are in space (and by that we mean geographical space).

---

*Being led by the assignments
of Heaven make for a richness
in one's life, because it's a spiritual
assignment that the spirit receives.*

> *The spirit gets the agreement of the soul and the body to carry it out.*

Living by the Function of the Spirit

The spirit must be forward and receiving the flow of Heaven to continue.

> *The assignments come and go —they are not static.*

They have a flow to them in time and space.

> *We can miss an assignment if we are not in the right timing.*

These assignments can be with others, with teams, or solo.

With the assignments of Heaven, we can get an assignment, or we can get an inclination of an assignment in a dream. We can get an inclination of an assignment by listening to Holy Spirit in our quiet time, in our journaling time, or by praying in tongues. If our spirit is focused on what Heaven is doing, even if our soul is in front doing something very necessary like caring for a child or caring for an elderly parent (our spirit knows when our soul is in front)—if our spirit is also focused on Heaven because we have had quiet time to get that assignment, then *during our day our spirit is connected with the Spirit of God.* Even when our soul is doing things, our spirit man is going to know when to break in to do an assignment.

Some of these assignments are prayer, or kindnesses, or the release of language to another human.

Living by the function of the spirit is another way to say this. This gets settled in our day when we open our day in some manner of seeking after God and giving ourselves permission that our spirit is going to abide with the Spirit of God all day. Also, we want our soul to give permission to our spirit to come forward and break through at any time.

Our soul and our spirit are divinely matched. They should work beautifully together in a flow of which one of them needs to be in operation in the moment.

The trouble is, for many humans, the distraction of the physical plane, the distraction of intentional distractions by world systems, and the capturing of the attention of the spirit through witchcraft, pharmakeia, wounding, and activity of demons—these things distract.

Let me explain what I mean by "capture our spirit." Our spirit is not captured, but **its *attention* is captured.** Its ability to flow with God—to thrive in His presence is captured. It is not ever away from us, so much as it is just turned to look at these other things that are gaining its attention. What happens is the soul compensates and the soul takes on a double-duty, trying to be the spirit *and* the soul.

The spirit of a man is refreshed in heavenly places, by the Spirit of God, and by ministering angels.

---
*The spirit can be disciplined
to dominate that person's life.*

It is a spiritual discipline. It is a work of pausing to determine what part of us should be working right now—our spirit, our soul, or our body. What part of us should be presenting up front right now? There are times of the day, times of the 24-hour clock, where it is really primed for our spirit to be receiving from Holy Spirit, and many do not do that. Therefore, many are sad. They are sick. They are hopeless. They are purposeless. This is because our assignment and our purpose come from Heaven.

---
*Little pieces of assignment
make up the whole of one's purpose.*

It flows in through one's lifetime—through the times of one's lifetime. There are times when it is seasons, it is cycles, it is times of the day, it is times of the week, times of the month, times of the year. It is where our blessing from Heaven is so available. If we will attune our spirit, we will receive.

These are also the times where the enemy is at work to deflect, divert, and disengage us from our primary life-giving moments of spirit to spirit, from operating and working from heavenly realms. So, the continuation of learning to live spirit-forward proceeds and must be practiced and advanced. When we feel stuck, we must learn to ask our angels to come near to help us, and they will.

Assignments can also come from messenger angels. These are for the mature saints. And by mature, I mean those who are several years on the planet, as well as the number of times spent in the presence of God and seeking heavenly realms. Wider portals are opening for this even now in the earth, wider portals and more saints operating from their spirit. And all of this is going to bring Heaven closer to earth.

Resistance

Changing subjects, I want to talk about resistance for a second.

> *Satan and his demons will work
> to resist us operating in our spirit.*

If we do not know that, we are going to let his lazy efforts keep us from being spirit forward. And he is *very* lazy.

The primary thing he will project to us is that *this is too hard*. The second thing he will use is *others are better than me at this. I will just leave it to them.* When we fall for these things, the kingdom of darkness wins in that moment. So, do not be like that.

Be assured and confident that we are competent, that we are a spirit being with this capacity. We have spiritual access to the Father, the Son, the Holy Spirit, angels, the cloud of witnesses, and heavenly realms. This is meant for us. Then practice, practice, practice. Make time to pause. It will be surprising to us that even if we pause for 10 minutes and seek the Kingdom for that 10-minutes, how it will change our morning or our afternoon, even amid clamoring distractions and natural things that have to be taken care of.

Here are some of the lies:

- I cannot do that.
- There is too much going on.
- I cannot do this now because I am no good at it.
- I can't pause and get into the Father's presence and be in spiritual realms even for 10 minutes, because there is no time.

These are some of the lies of the enemy and we must surmount them. We must overcome them. We must leap over them. Stand on top of them, rise over them, conquer them, and put them under our feet. See how small, inadequate, and piddly they are. Our practice doing that a couple of times in a row in a season is going to really help our soul step back, sit down, and rest. From doing that our spirit *and* our life will be enriched.

Quite honestly, we need to encourage each other in this. We need to encourage one another to be spirit forward. We need to talk about the enemy's lies and his distractions. We need to help each other understand when we have fallen into a pattern of being diverted, discouraged, or distracted, so we can encourage one another. We can encourage one another to break out by getting in the presence of God, getting in our secret place, and getting there in a consistent manner. Recognize that Heaven knows when we are attempting to do this, and Heaven is trying to help us. If we have time for 10 minutes or 15 minutes, that is much better than *no* minutes.

Let this be the biggest encouragement we give the Body of Christ. Two minutes, five minutes, 10 minutes, 18 minutes of being in heavenly places, seeking the Kingdom of God, and stepping into the realms of Heaven is so much better than *no* minutes.

Receive this word: "surmount," as in "I will surmount the distractions. I will surmount the diversions. I will surmount *and seek* the Kingdom of God."

---
*Surmount and seek
the Kingdom of God!*

Commission

I call the angels assigned to me to draw near.

[Await the sense of their arrival. Once we sense their arrival, verbally say:]

In the name of Jesus, I commission you to shield my realms from the lies of the enemy. I commission you to build a wall of fire above me, beneath me, and round about me on every side.

I commission you to tear down every stronghold and structure that exalts itself against the knowledge of God in my life.

Reading Our Scroll

In a recent testimony during our free weekly mentoring group, a lady mentioned that she commissions her angels to read her scroll to her continually. She also commissions the angels of her other family members, her spouse and children, to each read their scrolls to those family members. The repetition of hearing the scroll in our spirit continuously will aid us in fulfilling every aspect of our scroll. I encourage you to do so:

Commission to Read My Scroll

I call the angels assigned to me to come near.

[Await the sense of their arrival. Once you sense their arrival, verbally say:]

In the name of Jesus, I commission you to read to me continually the contents of my scroll so I may hear it, comprehend it with my spirit, and do it with diligence.

Summary

- Saints suffer because they lack seeking after the Kingdom of God.
- The sereneness of purpose is the subtraction of busy-ness.
- It is the flow of purpose.
- It has things to accomplish.
- It has places to be.
- It does not hold distraction.
- It does not hold busy-ness.
- It does not hold anxiety about the outcome.
- It holds faith and belief in a good outcome.
- Peace is a strength of Heaven, and we can engage this peace from our spirit, from our spirit man.
- We are not meant to fight against Leviathan, so let the angels of the Host fight through the angelic network.

- Remember, Leviathan is a defeated spirit.
- What humans do is they think about that spirit and forget that it is defeated, and it grows.
- The deception is that it will grow in their mind as an undefeated spirit when it is totally defeated.
- It knows it is defeated, but it is counting on the fact that we forget that
- Demons and princes project themselves as large and impenetrable, as impossible.
- We have a bigger projection than they do because we project from the realm of the Kingdom of God.
- Do not let the enemy project his largeness when he is little and under our feet.
- The people of God who are seeking the Kingdom are the ones who receive assignments.
- The people of God who have yet learned to seek for the Kingdom of God are not receiving assignments from Heaven.
- An assignment from Heaven can be known when we seek the Kingdom.
- We can step into realms of heaven and ask if there is an assignment for us, or
- Holy Spirit can give us the unction that we have an assignment.
- Assignments are activities—sometimes of words and sometimes a deed.
- Angels work to bring the peace of God to the earth.

- Saints can enter the Court of Records and find out if there is an assignment list and what is at the top.
- Assignments from Heaven come with timing.
- The spirit gets the agreement of the soul and the body to carry it out.
- Our soul and our spirit are divinely matched.
- Satan and his demons will work to resist us operating in our spirit.
- The primary thing he will project to us is that this is too hard.
- The second thing he will use is *others are better than me at this.*
- When we fall for these things, the kingdom of darkness wins in that moment.
- The repetition of hearing our angel read the scroll in our spirit continuously will aid us in fulfilling every aspect of our assignment.

Chapter 15

Using the Keys for Harvest

Our engagement with Heaven this day was brief. We had appealed to Ezekiel to come near, however, he was in the midst a battle and was unable to come at that moment.

In the meantime, we entreated Lydia to speak with us, and we learned that the angelic realm is busy. Commissioning angels continually is catching on with the Body of Christ, and it is good to commission our angels. Some of them are pleasantly at work for the first time in a long time. Some are new to their duties, having new networking skills with the angelic host and with Ezekiel, the ministry angel.

At that point, Ezekiel appeared having completed the battle he had been engaged in. We thanked him for coming and asked what weapons he needed.

By perception, we understood he needed weapons of warfare, and weapons for plundering. He also asked for assisting angels.

Ezekiel said, "These are not necessarily backup angels, but they are additional assistance for the ranks."

Father, we ask You in the name of Jesus, that the angel Ezekiel and his commanders be supplied with assisting angels for the ranks.

Specifically, he requested keys to doors underground, keys to doors under the earth, and keys for doors under the sea.

The sons and daughters of God in Jesus have not fully grasped that they have the keys that Jesus has.

We possess the same keys Jesus possessed.

The keys that Jesus has are ours. Many act like they are not.

The human race who is in Jesus Christ and yet alive on the earth have not realized that they have authority to use the keys that Jesus has, and He has ALL the keys.

Angels **do not** have the keys!

> *The sons and daughters*
> *of God have the keys.*

> *Angels can bring keys to the*
> *sons and daughters of God,*
> *or the sons and daughters of God*
> *can release keys to the angelic realm,*
> *to those angels that they have*
> *authority to work with.*

> *It is important to note that*
> *not every son and daughter*
> *has access to every key,*
> *but to the authority that*
> *they have been given by the King,*
> *they have keys to those things.*

These keys are not obtained by angels. They are obtained by the sons and daughters of God. These keys are for the express unlocking of new territories, the express unlocking of the wealth of the Father's warehouses and of the harvest, and also keys for the removal of veils—veils on God's people and on people who have not yet acknowledged the Lordship of Jesus Christ. These people are the wanderers. This grouping of people would be the ones that we call the lonely.

The lonely are those who are wandering, because they are operating from the emotion of being a lost one—not being connected or lost, as in they are not joined. We can release the keys of God's Kingdom to angelic hosts for the opening of doors and the removal of veils.

---

*Keys remove veils,
and keys also bring harvest.*

We were made to understand that by harvest, Heaven meant the wealth of the Kingdom and the timings of God's timing. We have the keys! We, the sons and daughters of God, have the keys and the ability to authorize angels to use those keys we have been given.

---

*We have the authority to authorize
the angels to use these keys.*

This ministry already has a key to a revelatory flow, and Ezekiel has been using that key for us. He also has a key to the new territory we have been given, and he is also showing us new territories. Now, he wanted the key to those not yet joined, and he wanted the commission to use that key to gather in harvest for those not yet joined. They are believers, but they are like lost sheep. They are disjoined from a group.

Father, I request on behalf of the angel Ezekiel, his commanders, and his ranks, weapons of warfare, that they be supplied with trebuchet,²² sledge, rope, listening devices, and binoculars.

I also request that the angel Ezekiel, his commanders, and his ranks be provided with weapons for plundering: sacks and sashes, keys to doors underground, keys to doors under the earth, and keys to doors under the sea.

I also request keys to those not yet joined because they are disjoined from a group. I ask these things be given to these angels, in the name of Jesus.

I also request angel elixir, angel food, and angel bread to be given to Ezekiel, his commanders, and his ranks.

I commission you, Ezekiel for the use of keys— keys to doors underground, keys to doors under the earth, keys to doors under the sea, keys to those doors and veils that have the need to be open so that people can join who are disjoined from a group, and keys to our territory.

I commission you to use these keys effectively to plunder the enemy's camp.

---

²² A type of catapult.

I also commission you to use your weapons of warfare to enforce the victory of the King, Jesus Christ and the Glory of the Father.

A scripture came to mind:

But now in Christ Jesus you who once were far off have been brought near by the blood of Christ. (Ephesians 2:13)

Commissioning for Our Angels:

I call the angels assigned to me to come near.

Father, I request on behalf of the angels assigned to me, keys.

I commission you for the use of keys—keys to doors underground, keys to doors under the earth, keys to doors under the sea, keys to those doors and veils that have the need to be open so that people can join who are disjoined from a group, and keys to the territory I steward.

I commission you to use these keys effectively to plunder the enemy's camp.

I also commission you to use your weapons of warfare to enforce the victory of the King, Jesus Christ and the Glory of the Father.

Summary

- The sons and daughters of God in Jesus have not fully grasped that they have the keys that Jesus has.
- We possess the same keys Jesus possessed.
- Angels do *not* have the keys!
    - The sons and daughters of God have the keys.
- Angels can bring keys to the sons and daughters of God, or
- The sons and daughters of God can release keys to the angelic realm, to those angels that they have authority to work with.
- It is important to note that not every son and daughter has access to every key, but to the authority that they have been given by the King, they have keys to those things.
- Keys remove veils and keys also bring harvest.
- We have the authority to authorize the angels to use these keys.

Chapter 16

The Hall of Treasures

As we engaged Heaven this day, at the Help Desk of the Business Complex we saw what we described as four-stacked small doors. They were stacked in twos and beside one another. It looked like safe deposit box drawers. Each door had a keyhole in it. These four doors were combined and joined into one rectangular metal box. This rectangular box was sitting on the countertop at the Help Desk.

Marcus, a man in white linen, spoke and informed us that what we were seeing was a representational vision of what has been unlocked and what is still locked as treasure from the storehouses of Heaven for our advancement. The Kingdom of Heaven has stored up for us some things locked, some things unlocked, but the revelation and the teaching of accessing those things in heavenly realms that have been unlocked are for us to understand now in a fresh manner. Some are things the Father has determined for us to be unlocked in His timing.

At this point we asked if we could all meet privately, as were standing in the lobby where the Help Desk was. We were taken to a small room, where we met to discuss these matters.

Marcus reminded us that there are things that are locked, things not yet unlocked, and things that are unlocked but have yet to be received. The receipt of the things that have been unlocked for us is what he wanted to talk about first. To receive what has been unlocked, first, we must have faith. *Faith is the key.* Some things have been unlocked to us, but we have not stepped into heavenly realms to access them.

---

*Some things are waiting for us,
but we must unlock them
in the heavenly realm.*

We have to intentionally pause to receive them. Jesus made this open for us. He owns every key and when we step into realms of Heaven, we can ask to see that which has been unlocked for us. Our experience of this can be a visual experience or experiential. These experiences can be numerous as well.

We often step in to ask what is in the Outstanding Folder, but...

> *We can also find in the Court of Records what has become unlocked for us as the seasons of time progress in the earth realm.*

This is tied to our maturing as sons and daughters of God. It is tied to the Father's events on earth. It is tied to the increase of His Kingdom on earth and the release of that increase. Do not be surprised that might and power from our Father in heavenly places can be received because a timed event has occurred where this has become unlocked.

Many suffer because they have not stepped into their understanding of access to the might and power that has been already released to the saints, and they simply have not come to get it unlocked. Then they have not released faith and belief to receive, but this can change. We will see it change dramatically in days ahead, the way the saints move upon the physical plane.

> *Religion and religious thoughts, which are those with an absence of God's determination to release His glory through His sons and daughters, will prevent us from pausing and considering how to receive what has been unlocked for us.*

There is an unlocking that has happened and that *will* happen that will unlock the treasures of our Father for their increase on earth. This requires spiritual thinking and the recognition of faith as the substance of that thing that is being unlocked.[23]

> *Wealth has been stored up and portions have been released and unlocked.*

At that point the scene changed, a long hallway could be seen. It was not very wide, but a little wider than a hallway in a home might be. The walls were not walls, however. They were rows and rows and rows and rows of what looked like safe deposit boxes. The boxes had names and numbers on them. They only have one keyhole for each, and it went on for a long distance. These are Treasure Boxes of Heaven. They are for the saints to receive. Angels come here when we assign keys to them, and they come and unlock things from this place.

We found a box that had "LifeSpring" written on it. It had one solid door, but when we opened that door there were four smaller doors like what was seen at the beginning of this engagement. The main or primary door had been opened for a long time. Of these inner doors the top two were closed. The bottom left door had a timer on

---

[23] Hebrews 11:1

it, and we had a key to the door of the bottom right box. It was an unlocking of a wealth resource.

By faith we responded to what we were seeing and said, "Thank You, Jesus for the key that you have created and given—this key made of light. I put this key of light into the lock of this right hand, bottom door. I insert it, and I open this door."

We could see currency—cash—in bundles. Also, there was a small decanter with a stopper in the top of it that had oil in it. The oil itself was really pretty. It was effervescent and milky looking. It looked like it was made of crushed sapphires or something similar, but it also had a milky substance. Imagine sapphires in a powder form mixed with a milky substance that was like cream. That is what it looked like.

We knew to take and receive what we were seeing by faith on behalf of LifeSpring International Ministries for Jesus' use—that His kingdom would come on earth as it is in Heaven. We learned that all of the things in all of these treasure boxes had scrolls attached to them.

We responded saying, "I also receive on behalf of LifeSpring International Ministries, its staff, its audience, its supporters, its viewers, and its listeners, these things for the increase of His Glory on earth, as it is in Heaven. By faith we receive it."

We learned that by faith we receive it, and by faith we can release it on earth because we have a trading floor. When we receive something in heaven and release it on earth, it multiplies because that is the principle of the Kingdom. Do this verbally by faith's release—verbally by faith.

---

*Our faith must be at
not just the receiving, but in
the releasing of multiplication.*

Seeing a butterfly, we realized we were learning to go in stages, just as a butterfly develops through stages.

When we release what has been stored up in places of Heaven that have been unlocked, then we receive it by faith. Then we release it by faith with focus, with intent, and with thoughts of "what would that be like?"—like shooting arrows at a target.

---

*Our release is when
we receive it in heavenly places.*

That would be like the caterpillar. We then release it into the earth realm. We have received it by vision, faith, and revelation. We then release it *verbally* with belief and faith and intent and focus, and it becomes like a butterfly.

The chrysalis stage is *in* our being. As we see by faith and hear by faith what is being released—this is the will of the Father. Then we are exchanging it within our being or our sphere or our realm and are releasing it with intent to others, for their receipt of it by faith. And like the chrysalis stage, when we release it verbally (with breath) into the physical realm, it becomes like the butterfly stage. It floats over or it wings its way to another who is a hearer of it by faith, and they receive it like a butterfly resting on their shoulder.

*[Pause right now and just begin to receive what has been released to **us** from Heaven.]*

The hardest part of this stage may be the coming here first to receive it by faith's sight,[24] discerning what is available, making the effort to sit down and engage Heaven, and be intentional. That is the hardest part because the work of Satan and his demons is *to keep us from the knowledge of our access here* and of *our identity in the physical plane from our spirit man*. Faith accesses the Light Key. Faith engages the Light Key. It is *not* the Light Key, but the key itself is light.

> *The spiritual activity is to step in and receive, unlock it, see what has been unlocked.*

When we look into the Treasure Box and see the cash and the oil, the overwhelming sense is just how rich our Father is. How wealthy and resource-filled the Father is, and how He desires to transfer this to His sons and daughters. Pray this:

---

[24] Faith always sees. It has sight.

I receive it by faith. I release it by faith. I release it by faith to those in my realms. Not only do I release it to them, but I release it to their households by faith.

I release the cash and the anointing oil to these and their households. I release it because it's the Father's good pleasure to give it. I have seen it by faith. I receive it by faith. I call the substance of it real.

I release increased financial cash flow, cash income, and multiplication to all these that I have mentioned. I also release the grace of the oil that flows with this cash. It goes together. I release the oil with it too.

The Oil of the Ease of Increase

We had just been introduced to a substance known as the Oil of the Ease of Increase. This oil has an aroma, and it attracts things. It attracts favor. It attracts multiplication. It attracts those moving in multiplication. This is done by faith. If we really got hold of how much substance faith has, it will change us eternally.

I release the Oil of the Ease of Increase to my family. I release it out of Your Kingdom. Father, glorify Your name as this oil is released and lights upon them, as it flows down upon them, as its aroma from the goodness of the Father of lights attracts increase into their lives, into their minds, into their being, into their body realm I release that in Jesus' name.

Whatever is lacking in their spirit realm, I release the Oil of the Ease of Increase to.

Whatever is lacking in their soul realm, I release the Oil of the Ease of Increase to.

To whatever is lacking in their body realm, I release the Oil of the Ease of Increase. Thank You, Father.

Marcus brought us back to a classroom and began to teach us that our enemy prowls around like a roaring lion seeking whom he may devour.[25] He desires to devour our faith. He desires to devour what we have released from the Father of lights. So, what we have released, we can release angelic help to protect.

> When the saints have knowledge of their own angels, they can commission their angels to protect that which has been released from Heaven and received.

I now ask my angels to come near.

---

[25] 1 Peter 5:8

[Wait until you sense their presence.]

I commission them to protect the Oil of the Ease of Increase for myself and my extended family.

I also release and commission my angels to protect the increase of cash, the increased cash flow multiplication.

I commission my angels to protect that as it has come from my Father into my realm. And I, by faith, will see it and move in it. I will utilize it. I will multiply it as it translates or manifests itself into physical things in my realms.

I request my angels to protect the manifestation of it, guard it, protect it from theft, protect it from destruction, protect it from being veiled to my sight and protect it as if they were protecting the glory of God—God's own glory.

I commission my angels to this task, in Jesus' mighty name.

I commission the angels that I have been talking about that are assigned to the people I have been releasing this to, to protect it in these ways as well.

I commission you to this in time and out of time, in the name of Jesus.

Having received this by faith, having guarded and protected that which we have been given, remember to multiply by spirit with thanksgiving the Oil of Ease of Increase.

I receive with thanksgiving, the increased wealth of cash coming to my sphere, my household sphere, my extended family members' spheres. I steward it. I watch over it.

I now have expectation to see it and the full circle comes when I see the manifestation of it. I give glory to God.

So, for physical increase, I declare right now by faith, I will have eyes to know. I will have eyes to see and a mind to know that this was the manifestation of that thing that I have gained from my Father by revelation and activity in His kingdom realm through Jesus, the door who gave me access to this place.

By doing this we have just done nothing less than what Jesus did when he multiplied the loaves and the fishes.

Father, I ask for grace to walk in this more. I also ask for angelic help so that the enemy cannot cap this. When I feel the pressing in of darkness to cap the goodness of God, to cap it or put a limit on it, and to say it cannot be that good, I receive the grace for that

I declare, it can be that good. God IS that good!

There is always enough. There's always another. There is no end in this. It cannot have an end because God has no end. It can't happen. It doesn't have to end. In the physical realm we think in terms of an end, but there is no end of this. It is quantifiably impossible for it to have an end.

If we just give glory to God and thank Him for what we have and what we are going to receive, then there is this activity of receiving by our spirit. It is an intentional activity to receive, and we *just do it by faith*. Be ready to be thankful, but also be ready to believe and know there is something else coming. This is not the end.

Engaging from Our Spirit

We asked Marcus to talk to us about the difference of our spirit engaging in all this and our soul engaging. We learned that there have been some who have engaged in this from their soul—this belief, this seeing like Abraham saw.[26] Abraham curated the vision of the promise of a son, of Isaac, in the spirit realm with his spirit, not his soul. He did it for a long time—but he did it, and he consistently did it.

---

[26] James 2:23, Galatians 3:6, Romans 4:3

> *Because he did it by faith*
> *with his spirit, he enjoyed Isaac*
> *as if Isaac was there.*

This is how to receive this.

> *Our spirit being has the capacity*
> *to be outside of time.*

We must see ourselves in the spirit realm, enjoying that thing that we are thinking on and believing God for. See that thing in the realms of Heaven. There's an important connection here between seeing, knowing, and receiving, and then enjoying it in spirit realms because our spirit is engaging it there.

It is almost like we are creating future memories from the spirit as we engage it. And then, when it manifests in the natural, it comes to the soul realm to now enjoy it. But we first enjoy it, embrace it, receive it, and I mean really engage it *from* our spirit.

Abraham engaged a little boy who was an heir that came from Sarah's womb, and he did it in the spirit. He did it by receiving the kindness of God, the goodness of God, and the quantity of purpose in it.

> *By faith our spirit can receive it*
> *and all its purpose as it apprehends it.*

Think of Abraham all those years with his soul desiring an heir, but *his spirit was already engaged* with the heir.

Satan wants to preach that God held out on Abraham all those years, but He didn't. Abraham was fully engaged in it. He did not know the timing of this manifestation until he was told by the angels that came to tell him that, but *he had already engaged*. This is why this makes so much sense. Then, with the near sacrifice of Isaac, we understand that Abraham had such a backstory with God, such a revelation of his powerful goodness, that if this is what the Father said to do, he could fully trust Him.

Abraham's statement that God will provide the sacrifice as they were going up the mountain in the story in Genesis 22 is a real key there. This was a lesson on our spirit's ability to receive—*our spirit's ability to be in faith*. That is what Marcus was contrasting for us, that many have tried this curation of the promise in the soul. Not only is the resistance hard there, but many times they are manufacturing from their soul the thing it is trying to *have faith for* instead of receiving from the realms of Heaven *from their spirit* the thing God is trying to give them.

[*Pause right now and ask: What is it God is trying to give me? What do I need to step into Heaven to receive what the Father has already stored up for me in His wealth storehouses or Treasure Boxes?*]

> *The things Heaven is giving are so available to be multiplied by our voice and our release.*

Commissioning of Ezekiel

Ezekiel, I would like to commission you. I have received an unlocking of the wealth of cash for the ministry and an Oil for Ease of Increase. I bless the Father for this.

I commission you Ezekiel, your commanders, and your ranks to protect the wealth of cash I have received, to protect and keep hidden from the enemy the Ease of Increase Oil that we have received, to help us distribute it to all the staff, all the supporters, and intercessors for all parts of LifeSpring International Ministries.

I commission you to protect it from destruction, protect it from theft, and protect it from being veiled from our sight. I commission you, the ranks, and your commanders to these things, in time and out of time, in the name of Jesus.

I thank You, Father, that angelic ranks are now released for this and have been commissioned for its protection, as it will glorify Your name. It will glorify Your worthiness, Your righteousness,

Your holiness, Your name that is above all other names.

We take hold of this as our rights as citizens of Heaven by covenant relationship with Jesus Christ. We rejoice for the increase of cash wealth and for the release of the Oil of the Ease of Increase for all who are connected to us.

I thank You for the lesson in faith. I thank You for the reminder of how to receive from spiritual realms the wealth of Your Kingdom as Jesus did. Even as Jesus did in His demonstration of the loaves and fishes, multiplying to not only to meet needs, but multiplying to glorify Your name, I thank You. I thank You that You interrupted the timeline of earth with Your glory through One who knew Himself as a Son and who was simply revealing to potential sons what You wanted to do. Thank You for that.

It is our sonship to believe and to engage by the spirit the release of this increase. As we enjoy it in the earth realm it is released to manifest in the natural plane and will arrive by the hands of angels.

How This Applies to Our Health

We can receive health by the spirit and walk in health by the spirit that our soul does not know about. It is a spiritual access when our spirit engages with the health of our body in the spirit realm, we can receive the health and the outworking of health to all our bodily systems there, all our circadian rhythms, all our hormonal rhythms—our entire being. It is all in Heaven. It is all available, but we must receive it *there* by faith in the spirit. We must engage *by our spirit man* our healthy body *there*, and we can discipline ourselves to focus on our healthy body *there* and the lack of pain that is in heavenly places that our spirit is able to feel like it's real there. Then, our spirit begins to translate that to our physical body. This is the changing of a flow of the mind in some manner, but we must receive it.

> We must receive the goodness of God
> by our spirit man first
> in the realms of Heaven.

When our spirit sees our spirit body in heaven, it sees a healthy body. It is virus free. It has virus defenses. It decodes with immediacy all viral code that would attempt to infiltrate the body. We are engaging this to the point of the manifestation of it in the physical realm. And the way it comes in, is we *say first with our spirit,* our *spirit must do this*—not our soul. Say,

> *I am not doing this from my soul because my soul gets weighed under its emotional anchors, but I free my spirit of those emotional anchors so my spirit can receive that healthy, COVID-free, COVID killing, COVID laughing-at body, and I am engaging it. It is a gift of my Father. It is made of light, and I am receiving it. I am wearing that*

body now. My physical body is a virus killing machine.

We have not even been bold enough to think about that because we have been laboring under what the physical realm contains right now, which is a lot of negative prophecy about how bad things are going to be. There is not going to be bad. *We* already have a body that is healthy. It is a *virus killing machine*.

A Quick Review

As a recap, what we found out is that we can go to the Court of Records and ask what has been unlocked for us. We found out that—for the ministry there was cash unlocked for us. We commissioned Ezekiel to preserve and protect and keep our eyes open, so it won't be veiled to us. We enjoy that by faith. We received the Oil of Ease of Increase as well for the ministry. This whole activity has increased the ministry by faith. It has increased the cashflow of this ministry by a lot, enabling us to touch more lives.

Later that day, I was approached by a team member with questions that just happened to have been answered by the engagement I just described. He and I engaged Heaven, and he went to the large hall (called the Hall of Treasures) and found his set of Treasure Boxes. He was granted permission to open all his boxes, so he received the key to each box. In his case one box contained property deeds. Another contained cash (in bundles wrapped with rubber bands) as well as jewelry and the vial of oil. In another box he discovered business contracts. All of this without any coaching by me. I let him describe what Heaven was unveiling. It was a joy to watch how closely his experience mirrored much of what was seen earlier.

Various nuances to the things people see can be expected when engaging the realms of Heaven. To one person an item might appear to be red in color, but to a different individual, it might appear totally different, but still be the same object. These distinctions can be expected, but none of the differences in interpretation invalidate what one person saw over the other. It is simply a matter of experience and interpretation. Religion would have us focus on the differences. Heaven suggests we focus on our similarities.

Releases & Commissionings

Release for Family

I release what has been unlocked for me today to my household. The Oil of the Ease of Increase, I release to my spouse. I release it to my daughter(s) and I release it to my son(s). I release it to my children's spouses and my grandchildren. I release it to my sister(s) and brother(s) and my brothers-in-law and sisters-in-law. I release it to my parents.

I release it out of Your Kingdom.

Father, glorify Your name as this oil is released, as it lights upon them, and as it flows down upon them. As its aroma from the goodness of the Father of lights attracts increase into their lives, into their minds, into their being, and into their body realm, I release that to fulfill its purpose in their lives. Whatever is lacking in their body realm, I release the Oil of the Ease of Increase to. I also ask this be done in time and out of time, in Jesus' mighty name. Thank You, Father.

Angelic Commissioning

I now ask my angels to come near.

[Wait until you sense their presence.]

I commission them to protect the Oil of the Ease of Increase for myself and my extended family.

I also release and commission my angels to protect the increase of cash and the increased cash flow multiplication*.

I commission my angels to protect that as it has come from my Father into my realm, and I, by faith, will see it and move in it. I will utilize it.

I will multiply it as it translates or manifests itself into physical things in my realms.

I want my angels to protect the manifestation of it, guard it, protect it from theft, protect it from destruction, protect it from being veiled to my sight, and protect it as if they were protecting the glory of God—God's own glory. I commission my angels to this task in Jesus' mighty name.

I commission the angels that I have been talking about that are assigned to the people I have been releasing this to, to protect it in these ways as well, in the name of Jesus.

I receive with thanksgiving, the increased wealth of cash coming to my sphere, my household sphere, my extended family member's spheres. I steward it. I watch over it. I now have expectation to see it, and the full circle comes when I see the manifestation of it. I give glory to God for physical increase.

I declare right now by faith I will have eyes to know. I will have eyes to see and a mind to know that this was the manifestation of that thing that I have gained from my Father by revelation and activity in His kingdom realm through Jesus, the door who gave me access to this place.

* What has been unlocked for others may be different. Access the Court of Records and request to know what has been unlocked.

Summary

- The Kingdom of Heaven has stored up for me some things locked, some things unlocked.
- Some are things the Father has determined for me to be unlocked in His timing.
- Faith is the key.
- Some things have been unlocked to us, but we have not stepped into heavenly realms to access them.
- We have to intentionally pause to receive them.
- Jesus made this open for us.
- He owns every key and when we step into realms of Heaven, we can ask to see that which has been unlocked for us.
- We can also find in the Court of Records what has become unlocked for us as the seasons of time progress in the earth realm.
- It is tied to the increase of His Kingdom on earth and the release of that increase.
- Many suffer because they have not stepped into their understanding of access to the might and power that has been already released to the saints and they simply have not come to get it unlocked.
- Religion and religious thoughts, which are those with an absence of God's determination to release His glory through His sons and daughters, will prevent us from pausing and

considering how to receive what has been unlocked for us.
- When we receive something in heaven and release it on earth, it multiplies because that is the principle of the Kingdom.
- Our faith must be at not just the receiving, but in the releasing of multiplication.
- The spiritual activity is to step in, receive, unlock it, and see what has been unlocked.
- Our spirit being has the capacity to be outside of time.
- See ourselves in the spirit realm, enjoying that thing that we are thinking on and believing God for.
- By faith our spirit can receive it and all its purpose as it apprehends it.
- The things Heaven is giving are so available to be multiplied by our voice and our release.
- It is our sonship to believe and to engage by the spirit the release of this increase.
- As we enjoy it in the earth realm, it is released to manifest in the natural plane and will arrive by the hands of angels.
- We must receive the goodness of God by our spirit man, first in the realms of Heaven.

Chapter 17

Commission for Ripened Harvest

On this morning, we met with George, a man in white who serves as our financial advisor for the ministry.

George wasted no time instructing us this day. He began, "**It's time to announce an upward trend. It's time to announce an upward financial trend. It's time to announce a turning point at the gate.** It's time to announce, because we are in the new year gate. We are in the gate of the new year—the threshold of the new year. Our seed has been sown and harvest awaits. It's time to release the laborers to those fields to bring in the harvest. This harvest is not the salvation harvest. This harvest is a financial harvest. It is an increase in portion.

It is an increase in the things, people, connections, and opportunities that result from increased harvest.

Then, that results in harvest harvested and stored in storehouses.

We have the Right of Inheritance.

Release the harvesters—they are angels to be released into our harvest fields—the harvest fields of the ministry.

It was explained to me that it was a two-fold activity.

(1) Release angels to clean up the tares and remove them from our harvest field.
(2) Then release angels to gather in the ripened harvest as increase to be stored in our warehouses.

These wheat fields are ripened and waiting. They are ripened to harvest. It translates to all the things you know your ministry is involved with and should be doing. It equates to personnel, opportunity, signed contracts, ease of movement, the release of anointed friendships—friendships for the purpose of scattering more seed.

When we release angels to these works, remember the cycle of seed, time, and harvest for we need to harvest so we have seed. This is the Father's goodwill for us. This is the blessing of God for His children, that they harvest seed and harvest the multiple harvests of the seed as it is the multiplication of His Kingdom.

The Commission

We can commission them because we have both spiritual seed and physical seed. The physical seed that we have sown is like money—currency, but it has also been time.

Time is the pouring out of our life, which is the release of seed.

I commission, in the name of Jesus, the harvesting angels to fill their sacks with the ripened seed, to bring it securely to the storehouse and to cause it to be stored there for the manifestation of increase in these different forms of the multiplication of the King's Kingdom: opportunities, time, friendships, finances, and all the things we have been discussing with George. I agree with those things to be harvested.

I also commission you, in the name of Jesus, to pluck up tares from our fields and to remove them and then put them in the trash.

[At that point the angels had a hoe in their hands.]

I commission you to use that hoe, to pluck up tares, remove them from our fields, and see that they are done away with.

I commission you at the head of this year for this coming year to be consistently and always on this task on behalf of LifeSpring International Ministries on behalf of all its staff and their households, on behalf of all the supporters and those who do trade with us, and those who are our clients and their households.

I also commission you to pay special attention to that area of the earth known as Pinehurst, North Carolina.

As you harvest the ripened seed, I also commission you to tie up your sacks securely with these belts, so that nothing is lost as you bring them to the storehouse for LifeSpring International Ministries and these I have mentioned.

So now, I set a decree. I agree with the expansion of the King's Kingdom. I agree that LifeSpring International Ministries will be a full storehouse, a full warehouse, a full barn, and that we will have more than enough, plenty to share, and much to rejoice over.

What we heard was a type of prophecy—a type of a prophetic word, but it came from the Spirit of the Lord out of the King to the expansion of His Kingdom. This is how we create; this is one of the ways we create grace.

Chapter 18
Commissioning Angels Script

I invite the angels assigned to me to draw near.

In the name of Jesus, I commission you, to perform sentry duty at all my gates, to disallow entry from anything not written in the books of Heaven about me, and to allow entry for everything that is.

I also commission you to patrol my bridges—the bridges of my relationships, the bridges of my spirit, soul, and body, to disallow anything not written about me in the books of Heaven, and to allow in and gather those things that are.

I commission you to block up every illegal access point.

I also commission you to thoroughly search my realms and find every interloper and intruder and *to deal with them to cause them to exit, in Jesus' name*.*

[*The only thing that will not respond to that is a lingering human spirit (LHS).]

Chapter 19

Angels of Advancement

This last chapter describes the Angels of Advancement, who do not need a commissioning as they already have their marching orders from the Father. We had been engaging Heaven concerning Business Advocate Services Global[27] and Heaven had begun speaking of **a new movement of young entrepreneurs**[28] that was breaking forth in the earth.

Lydia, who had been teaching us asked, "Can you have faith for it in that degree? Can you see it in the spirit and call it in at that degree?

We learned that the trading of these types of businesses are the advancement of the Kingdom through the hands of warring angels who trample the enemy out of these angels' incredible victory and the power they

---

[27] Now known as Heaven Down Business, Inc. Visit the website at: HeavenDownBusiness.com
[28] See the article, "New Realm of Young Entrepreneurs" at CourtsOfHeavenWebinars.com

receive from their initiation rites from the King. These are the angels reserved for this time. They are marked with the word *Advance* and are known as Advancing Angels.

> *We need Advancing Angels for **maximum impact** in the society.*

Advancing Angels are in likeness, somewhat fierce. And they are extremely focused. They don't put up with the immature sons of God very well. They lay steppingstones for the group, organization, or individual who has decided that they will no longer have anything to do with the world and its systems, but will advance into the demonstration of the Glory of God.

Advancing angels have been released to every nation on earth. They come at specific times of the year, more so than others, yet they are available now. Advancing angels greet the believer who is hungry with great joy.

Advancing angels are equipped with very large, piercing arrows. They know when to use them.

> *They do NOT need a commission.*

They also have what looks like wings on their ankles, like the depiction of the mythical Mercury in Greek mythology. These advancing angels have something to do with times, and they have been anxiously awaiting their time. They have repeatedly requested of the Father for their release.

They are drawn to those who operate in *courage and boldness*. They are also drawn to those who have laid down pretty much everything to be spiritual son of God. They are drawn to those who think in terms of victory. They are also drawn to those whose mindsets are to live from principles of the Kingdom in which there is nothing impossible. There is faith for everything. There is enough faith and belief—primarily in the unseen realm, and that accomplishes things on behalf of the natural.

The company of Advancing Angels are the angels that we are looking for. These are the angels that we need, these Advancing Angels—the Angels of Advancement—because the final goal in their mind is *the advancement of the Kingdom of God to make it seen on physical earth as they see it in Heaven.*

How do we receive these Advancing Angels? We make our requests known to God, but we should be ready. We should prepare our soul to follow our spirit. We can prepare our spiritual senses to speak to our spirit, to translate to our soul realm what the Spirit of God is doing. The mind, following after the *soul only*, will resist what Advancing Angels are prepared to accomplish. The soul and mind must become comfortable with change—even rapid change. Mostly the soul must become comfortable with **not being able to control something** but rather to enjoy the process of what the spirit is covenanted to.

> *The soul must
> become comfortable
> with not being able
> to control something*

The soul has an expectation that things will not change, but the status quo—what is, will be improved. However, the soul does not want it to improve to the point of change, to the point of looking different, feeling different, smelling different, or operating differently. So, the soul will think, "Yeah, I want change," but it wants change *only in increments that it can control.*

Advancing angels will change a landscape, a nation, a group of people, an organization with such a rapid amount of change that the soul will be panting. Then the soul's only recourse will be to rest and learn its place of rest, so that the Kingdom of God is displayed.

The soul must be prepared for persecution. There will be great resistance to those who operate with Advancing Angels. If the soul is ready to flex, if the soul is ready to be second, if the soul is ready to not hold on to preconceived ideas of how a thing should or should not play out—should or should not be, if the soul is ready to stand aside and watch the power of the Spirit of God in conjunction with our spirit, THEN we **will** demonstrate the Kingdom of God on earth. It will supersede time. We call these miracles. It will supersede the ability of the soul. It will cause what is "in Heaven" to be experienced by the soul and the mind in the physical realm, even though the soul and the mind did not play a part in its coming to pass.

The Father is waiting on sons who will make room for this. Allow for this. Desire, hunt, and want this. It will break apart every paradigm of what the soul thought it was doing. And it will enliven the spirit with joy.

These Advancing Angels have been seen on planet earth before by the naked eyes of men. These were the angels that spoke to the shepherds on the night that Jesus was brought forth. These were the representatives of the advancement of the Kingdom, the advancing of the Father's manner of His expression, and His next step of His plan. As the heart of the shepherds tried to grasp an understanding around what really happened—which was the breaking forth of a contingent of angels—no wonder the shepherds were sore afraid.[29] We forget that in the story.

Ezekiel's Understanding

With that, Lydia had completed her engagement. We then asked Ezekiel to draw near, and he mentioned upon his arrival that he has knowledge of these Advancing Angels. He said, "I know of their rank." He cautioned us, saying, "Listen to Lydia. Hear what she said."

We learned from Ezekiel that these Advancing Angels can be fearsome, but they are not to be feared like we are

---

[29] Luke 2:9

afraid of them, because our identity as a son of God causes them to rejoice. These angels are very timed. They have a real strong connection with times that come from Heaven, the times that are in each generation, but there are more Advancing Angels released from Heaven to the realm of the spirit on earth than before.

We realized these angels were a bit different than the ranks of angels that we have become accustomed to. These angels listen to what the Godhead says. They are very timed in that. These Advancing Angels carry a frequency about them that contains the fear of the Lord, which is where their awesomeness comes from—their fierceness comes from. Therefore, they don't put up with much. They have eyes to see sons of God who are matured and maturing.

They were not designed to be the angels that work with those who are infants in their journey.

There is a sonship status quo that we press into that highlights us to these angels.

Ezekiel mention that they are very aware of the hidden Books of Heaven. They have knowledge he does not have. Advancing Angels are essentially a different ranking of angel.

With that statement, our engagement with the realms of Heaven was over. We had learned of an entirely new ranking of angels that we prepared our hearts to request of the Father. Remember, these angels do not tolerate immaturity well and are for those who are sons or who are maturing into their sonship with the Father. Be a responsible steward of these mighty ones of God.

Father, we receive the Angels of Advancement into our realms and into the realms of LifeSpring International Ministry. We thank You for their work and welcome their working in behalf of the Kingdom of God.

Chapter 20
Conclusion

The encouragement to commission our angels to assist us was outlined in Chapter 1. As you have read this book you have had many opportunities to commission your angels. You will have found your life much richer as you have learned to co-labor with these ministering spirits sent by the Father to let you know you are loved 24/7, 365 days a year.

The information and exhortations within this book, I hope, will become a regular part of your spiritual walk. Angels desire to work with us as we extend the Kingdom of Heaven into the earth. They are simply awaiting the voice of His Word (Psalm 103:20). As we shed old ideas and misconceptions of these mighty ministers of the Lord, we will be able to embrace more fully what they do and how they do it.

We have experienced the benefits of commissioning our angels many times since we learned of this concept. The commissions included in the book were those we used as we were in the moment. Heaven has given clear instruction to me to obey quickly any instructions given. One of those instructions was to release revelation quickly once we received it from Heaven. We have sought to obey that instruction, as many of the chapters were released as blog posts on CourtsOfHeavenWebinars.com prior to being compiled into this book.

Part of our calling is to disseminate revelation to the Body of Christ to grow up the sons in this hour. Our Platinum Members have experienced that often, as many times Heaven has shared with us on Wednesday at 10AM and instructed us to deliver it to the Platinum Members at our 12:00 Noon (Eastern time) meeting that same day. The freshness of the revelation has a cutting edge that slices through traditions and beliefs that would otherwise hold us back in our maturing walk with God.

I encourage you to not waste your time trying to convince those whose ear has not been prepared to hear or whose eyes have not been prepared to see. It will frustrate all the parties involved. We will find hearers and seers as we journey along. Work with the hungry. We can't fill a full vessel.

Remember, the thirsty
will seek out water
and the hungry will
seek out nourishment.

The revelation you now carry, I encourage you to now ruminate and meditate on. As you are reading and re-reading this book and others we produce, pray in the spirit so you maximize the reception of the revelation to your spirit and eventually to your soul. Remember, the soul is not designed to be the initial container for revelation. It will gain the information later as it can handle it.

Now, follow me in this final commission for your angels:

I call the angels assigned to me to draw near.

[Wait until you sense their presence.]

In the name of Jesus, I commission you to cause the intake of revelation from this book to be watered and cultivated so it brings forth maximum fruit in my life, in my family, in my relationships, and in my business, ministry, or employment arena.

Thank you for your diligent service for the Kingdom.

May you experience new levels of protection, provision, and growth as you live the principles of this book. God bless you richly.

Appendix

Learning to Live Spirit First

A challenge with how we were taught about the Christian life is that everything was put off until sometime in the future. Then, we read the letters of Paul and we experienced a disconnect. Heaven, to us, was a destination, not a resource. We knew nothing about learning to live from our spirits. We only knew what we had been doing all our lives since birth, and that is to live to satisfy our soul or our flesh. We sorely need to learn an alternative way of living.

Exchanging Our Way of Living

Paul recorded these words in his letter to the Romans:

Those who are motivated by the flesh only pursue what benefits themselves. But those who live by the impulses of the Holy Spirit are motivated to pursue spiritual realities. (Romans 8:5)

We must learn to live spirit first! We must exchange our way of living. We must learn to live from our spirit. We need to understand the hierarchy within us:

- We are a spirit.
- We possess a soul.
- We live in body.

Each component has a specific purpose in our lives. Our spirit is the interface with the supernatural realm. It is designed for interfacing with Heaven and the Kingdom realm. Our spirit has been in existence in our body since conception. Our soul has a different purpose. It communicates to our intellect and our physical body what our spirit has obtained from Heaven. It is the interface with our body. Our body houses the two components and will follow the dictates of whichever component is dominating,

Most of us have never been taught about having our spirit dominate. Rather, we have merely assumed that our soul being dominant was the required mode of operation.

Our soul always wants to be in charge. Our soul is susceptible to carnal or fleshly desires, lusts, and behaviors. It will, at times, resist our spirit and body. It must be made to submit to our spirit by an act of our will.

Our will is a means of instructing either component (spirit, soul, or body) what to do. Our soul has a will and so does our spirit. We choose who dominates!

Our body, on the other hand, has appetites that will control us in subjection to our soul. They become partners in crime—remember that second piece of chocolate cake it wanted? Our body will try, along with our soul, to dictate our behavior. It will likely resist the spirit's domination of our life. However, it will obey our spirit's domination if instructed, and our body can aid our spirit if trained to do so.

The typical expression that operates in most people's lives is that their soul is first, body second, and their spirit is somewhere in the distance in last place.

In some people, especially those very conscious of their physical fitness or physical appearance, there is a different lineup. Their body is their priority, the soul second, and again their spirit is the lowest priority.

Heaven's desire for us is vastly different. Heaven desires that we live spirit first, soul second, and body third. Since we are spiritual beings, this is the optimal arrangement. For most of us, our spirit was not activated in our life in any measure until we became born again.

If, after our salvation experience, we began to pursue our relationship with the Father, then we became much more aware of our spirit and learning to live more spirit conscious. The apostle Paul wrote in his various epistles about living in the spirit or walking in the spirit.

> *Because we are spiritual beings,
> our spirits cry out for a deepening
> of relationship with the Father.*

Our spirit longs for it and will try to steer us in that direction.

Our soul has certain characteristics that explain its behavior in our life. This is the briefest of lists, but I think we will get the idea. Our soul is selfish. It wants what it wants when it wants it. It can be very pouty. It can act like a small child. It is offendable and often even looks for opportunities to be offended. Our soul is also rude.

Our body has a different set of characteristics. It is inconsiderate, demanding, lazy, and self-serving. It does not want to get out of bed in the morning, for many people. In others, it wants to be fed things that are not beneficial.

However, characteristics of our spirit are hugely different. If we live out of our spirit, we will find that we are loving and prone to be gentle. We desire peace. We are considerate. We are far more contented when living out of our spirit. Also, joy will often have great expression in our lives.

Sometimes, we have experienced traumas that create a situation of our soul not trusting our spirit. The soul blames the spirit for not protecting it. The irony is that typically, our soul never gave place to the spirit so that it could protect us. The soul places false blame on the spirit, and it must be coerced to forgive the spirit. Then the soul must relinquish control to the spirit. Once the soul forgives the spirit, the two components can begin to work in harmony.

If I were to flash an image of some delicious, freshly cooked donuts in front of us, what would happen? For many, their body would announce a craving for one. What if, instead, I showed an image of a bowl of broccoli? How many people would get excited about that? Probably not as much excitement over a bowl of broccoli would be exhibited. Which does our body prefer—the donuts or the broccoli? For the untamed soul, the donuts are likely to win out every time. Which do most kids prefer?

In any case, we can train ourselves to go for the healthier option. A principle regarding this that I heard years ago, is summed up like this:

What we feed will live—
what we starve will die

What do we want to be dominant—our spirit, our soul, or our body? The part we feed is the part that will dominate.

For some, they feed their soul and live by the logic of their mind. Everything must be reasoned out in their mind before they will accept it. However, because our soul gains its insight from the Tree of the Knowledge of

Good and Evil, it will always have faulty and limited understandings.

How do we change this soul-dominant or body-dominant pattern? We instruct our soul to back up and we call our spirit to come forward. Some people may need to physically stand up and speak to our soul and say, "Soul, back up," and as they say those words, take a physical step backward. Then, speak to their spirit out loud and say, "Spirit, come forward." As we speak those words, take a physical step forward. This prophetic act helps trigger a shift within them.

Live spirit first!

Benefits of Living Spirit First

Why would we want to live spirit first? Let me present several reasons. Living spirit first will create in us an increased awareness of Heaven and the realms of Heaven. It will create a deeper comprehension of the presence of Holy Spirit, of angels, and men and women in white linen. We will be able to better hear the voice of Heaven. We will experience greater creativity, productivity, hope, and peace. We will become more aware of the needs of people that we meet.

As we live spirit first, we will be able to access the riches of Heaven in our life. Petty things that formerly bothered us will dissipate in importance or impact in our life. We will be able to move ahead, not concerned with the petty, mundane, or unproductive things that have affected our life before we began to live spirit first.

This way of life is more than a game changer—for the believer, it is the only way to live. We will face challenges as we build our business or live our life from Heaven down, but we will more readily be able to access the solutions of Heaven as we live with an awareness of the richness of Heaven and all that is available to us as a son or daughter of the Lord Most High. Do not live dominated by the soul. *Live **spirit** first!*

Works Cited

Simmons, B. (2018). *The New Testament (The Passion Translation)*. BroadStreet Publishing Group, LLC.

Strong, J. (n.d.). *Strong's Concordance*.

Description

Maximizing Our Relationship
with Heavenly Hosts

Many in the army of the Lord, meaning the sons and daughters of God, do not have an understanding of the spiritual nature of the King. They are working from the realm of the soul to do the work of the Kingdom. They must soon learn the engagement of spiritual things in the spirit realm, from their spirit, for this is their weapon of war.

Put angels to work. Commission them often. Supply them with weapons. Believe in their strength. Our belief in what they do is a form of belief in who our Father is, in His position as Almighty God, and in the blueprint of His plans. The necessary posture of prayer in these times requires the ministry of angels in spiritual realms.

Learning to commission our angels is vital to helping them fulfill their role in our behalf. We are meant to work with angels and the only way to grow is to practice.

About the Author

Dr. Ron Horner is an apostolic teacher specializing in the Courts of Heaven. He has written over twenty books on the Courts of Heaven, engaging Heaven, working with angels, or living from revelation.

He currently trains people in engaging the Courts of Heaven in a weekly online teaching session. You can register to participate and discover more about the Courts of Heaven prayer paradigm from his various websites, classes, products, and services found here:

www.ronhorner.com

Other Books by Dr. Ron M. Horner

Building Your Business from Heaven Down

Building Your Business from Heaven Down 2.0

Cooperating with The Glory

Courts of Heaven Process Charts

Dealing with Trusts & Consequential Liens from the Courts of Heaven

Engaging Angels in the Realms of Heaven

Engaging Heaven for Revelation – Volume 1

Engaging Heaven for Revelation – Volume 2

Engaging Heaven for Trade

Engaging the Courts for Ownership & Order

Engaging the Courts for Your City (*Paperback, Leader's Guide & Workbook*)

Engaging the Courts of Healing & the Healing Garden

Engaging the Courts of Heaven

Engaging the Help Desk of the Courts of Heaven

Engaging the Mercy Court of Heaven

Four Keys to Dismantling Accusations

Freedom from Mithraism

Kingdom Dynamics – Volume 1

Let's Get it Right!

Lingering Human Spirits

Lingering Human Spirits – Volume 2

Living Spirit Forward

Overcoming the False Verdicts of Freemasonry

Overcoming Verdicts from the Courts of Hell

Releasing Bonds from the Courts of Heaven

Unlocking Spiritual Seeing

www.ingramcontent.com/pod-product-compliance
Lightning Source LLC
Chambersburg PA
CBHW022005160426
43197CB00007B/286